YOGA

FOR THE FAMILY

ISBN: 978-81-7436-826-3

Editors: Neeta Datta, Diya Koshy
Design: Arati Subramanyam
Layout: Kumar Raman
Production: Naresh Nigam

This edition Roli & Janssen BV 2011
Published in India by Roli Books
in arrangement with Roli & Janssen BV
M-75, Greater Kailash-II Market
New Delhi–110 048, India.
Phone: ++91-11-4068 2000
Fax: ++91-11-29217185
Email: info@rolibooks.com
Website: www.rolibooks.com

Printed and bound in Singapore

YOGA

FOR THE FAMILY

A HOLISTIC APPROACH

BHARAT THAKUR

Lustre Press
Roli Books

CONTENTS

WHY YOGA FOR THE FAMILY

Yoga means togetherness of awareness and body. It is a practical science aiming at the realization of the ultimate—moksha.

The purpose of this book is to remove the misconception that yoga is for the elderly and the sick. The practice of yoga should ideally be commenced in early childhood when the body is, by nature, loose and flexible. Beginning early brings truth to the old adage 'prevention is better than cure'. Though yoga does help in the treatment of disease, this is not its only goal.

Ancient masters like Patanjali have made mankind aware of the fact that yoga is a science which is practical and usable with guaranteed scope of growth at all levels of human existence—physical, mental, emotional, psychological, and spiritual. Its sole principle is to progress from a state of doing to the state of non-doing.

The ancient art of yoga says that an empty mind is God's workshop.

With the passage of time, medical sciences have made tremendous progress. So have metaphysics, physics, chemistry, human physiology, and sports medicine. Yoga, which is a practical science, however, has fallen into the hands of those who don't really understand its depth and use it for superficial purposes such as figure-correction, weight loss, and stress management.

You may wonder: 'I know a few asanas (postures), *bandhas* (neuromuscular locks), mudras (gestures), and *kriyas* (purification techniques). When I practise them, all I feel is relaxed and light.'

It is your inability to get involved at deeper levels that blocks yoga's ability to take you beyond relaxation and a feeling of lightness. The mad materialistic race for earning more than what you need, the latest cars and cellphones has made you so busy, that you forget that with every breath, you are closer to death.

Yoga is not only a science that can be used as a curative to relax and de-stress you, but one that aids in understanding life, and can be used by a logical mind to go beyond logic. It allows a person who has given in to lust, greed, and desire to gain freedom from the senses. To some, this could mean death. However, the first lesson of yoga is withdrawal from the senses—*pratyahaar*.

Yoga is a systematic growth ladder that begins with *yama* and *niyama* (the basic ethical codes of life), asana to master the body and pranayama to go beyond the body. These constitute *bahirang* (external) yoga and the *antarang* yoga (inward journey) that begins by experimenting with the senses (*pratyahaar*), which helps achieve tranquility; and a new world begins. External yoga has the effect of a mother's lullaby. It helps soothe the child to sleep. While sleep helps the practitioner achieve a tranquil state, the song makes him unafraid, stable, and comfortable with his eyes closed. From here the new world begins.

The practitioner continues by experimenting with the second step—*dharana* (thought and absence of thought). Success in this is a state of bliss—relaxed, awakened and a genuine sense of freedom from all attachment, pain and joy, a shift from ego to egolessness, from skepticism to surrender, and from falling in love to happiness within. This is *dhyana* (profound meditation), the third step in the internal journey. After this, he starts experimenting with happiness. Then the last door opens. The untold, unheard, unsaid and unknown reveals its own presence. He embarks with his awakened consciousness on a journey leading to the ultimate conquest of the fear of death.

Yoga for the Family is my effort for you. I would like you to start enjoying the drugged-like effect of stretching and the addictive practice of external yoga which may lead you someday to the last door of knowledge.

The body is an amazing machine—the only machine in the universe that converts bread to blood. The five elements (earth, water, fire, air, and ether) that make up the universe are combined in the human body. Light is the source of energy, just as heat is the source of human energy. The man who knows the secrets of his own body will surely know the secrets of the universal consciousness.

Scientists have researched our bodies and developed equipment to measure different parameters of the output of their experiments. The ancient Indian yogis studied the human body and have came with the amazing knowledge of the *nadi* system. *Nadis* are a network of electrical pathways inside the human body and the yogis discovered that if there is any pause or 'short circuit', the body becomes sick or experiences loss of movement in that joint in the form of edema, pain, and so on. Yogis classified the air present in the body as *prana*, *apana*, *samana*, *vyana*, and so on. They developed ways to remove unwanted air and improve the condition of the body. They called it *pranayama*.

Yogis differentiated areas of the body and named them *khandas* or *lokas*. They developed a system called asana to balance and optimize strength, mobility, and fluidity of the limbs.

To cleanse the interiors of the body on a daily basis, they developed *shatkarmas* or *kriyas* that begins with the eyes, nasal passage, and alimentary canal. Yogis also developed asanas to remove blockages in the blood vessels; by inverting their body and standing on their heads, yogis used the gravitational pull to enhance blood circulation in the upper section of the body—the *mastishk* (head).

The practice of yoga enhances the body's strength, resilience, and general health, without aggressive interference in its natural internal processes. Thus, yoga can be described as the ultimate medicine for ailments of the human body because it helps one to make the shift from dependence on the physical attributes to a mental or intellectual state of existence.

YOGA FOR THE BODY

BENEFITS

Loosens spinal vertebrae.

Massages the abdomen and digestive organs; effective in removing wind and constipation.

CAUTION

Not to be performed by people with serious back conditions such as sciatica and slipped disc.

PAWANAMUKTASANA

SINGLE LEG LOCK

1

Lie flat on your back. Fold your right knee and grasp it with your hands.

2

Pull your knee down towards your chest

3

Lock your knee to your chest. Raise your upper body till your chin touches your knee. Hold for 20-30 seconds, release your leg and lie down.

PAWANAMUKTASANA

LEG LOCK

1

Lie flat on your back. Bend your knees and place your feet on the floor.

2

Interlock your hands around your knees and pull them down towards your chest

3

Draw your knees completely down to the chest and touch your chin to the knees. Hold this posture for 20-30 seconds and then release your legs and lie down.

BENEFITS

Loosens spinal vertebrae.

Massages the abdomen and digestive organs; effective in removing wind and constipation.

CAUTION

Not to be performed by people with serious back conditions such as sciatica and slipped disc.

BENEFITS

Relieves strain of driving and desk work.

Helps relieve cervical spondylitis and frozen shoulders.

Tones the muscles of the chest and shoulders.

PAWANAMUKTASANA

SHOULDER SOCKET ROTATION

1

Sit comfortably with your back straight. Fold your elbows and place your fingertips on your shoulders.

2

Rotate your shoulders. Repeat five times. Then reverse the direction and repeat five times.

PAWANAMUKTASANA

WRIST CLENCH

1

Sit comfortably with your back straight. Stretch your arms out and clench your fists.

2

Release your fists and stretch your fingers out. Repeat ten times.

BENEFITS

Improves circulation in the forearms.

Relieves stress.

Tones muscles of the forearms.

BENEFITS

Relieves tension in the neck and shoulders.

Relieves stress from desk work.

Helps to prevent cervical spondylitis.

CAUTION

People with cervical spondylitis should do this gently.

PAWANAMUKTASANA

NECK ROTATION

1

Sit comfortably with your back straight. Drop your head down.

2

Gently rotate your neck in a complete circle. Repeat this procedure five times. Then practise five times in the reverse direction.

PAWANAMUKTASANA

KNEE PRESS

1

Sit comfortably with your back straight and legs stretched out in front. Bend your right leg at the knee and pull it in with both hands; press against your trunk.

2

Pull your left leg in. Hold both legs pressed tightly. Then release your legs. Repeat five times.

BENEFITS

Frees the knee joint.

Helps in opening up the groin area.

Helps in relieving knee pain.

SURYA NAMASKAR

SUN SALUTATION

BENEFITS

Stretches and strengthens every muscle in the body and increases flexibility.

It is a complete cardio-respiratory exercise co-ordinating physical movement with breath.

Balances the homeostasis (internal hormonal environment) and revitalizes the body, filling it with energy.

Helps the body lose weight and, more importantly, maintain itself, preventing it from regaining the lost weight.

1

Stand straight, join your palms in front of your chest. Inhale. Bend backwards and stretch your hands back keeping your palms joined.

2

Exhale. Bend your body down and touch your palms to the floor, and forehead to your knees. Keep your knees straight.

3

Inhale. Bend one leg and place your foot forward, between your hands. Stretch your other leg to the back and bend your back, looking upwards.

CAUTION

Should not be practised by people suffering from acute cases of high blood pressure, heart diseases, and those who have had a stroke.

Should be avoided by people with hernia.

People with acute back conditions should approach *surya namaskar* cautiously and discontinue if the condition is aggravated.

Should not be practised during fevers and inflammations.

Should be avoided during the onset of menstruation.

4

Exhale. Take your forward leg back and keep your body straight and stable, the body weight balanced on your toes and palms.

5

Hold your breath (no inhalation). Drop your knees and then your chest and chin to the floor. Raise your hips up.

Yoga is not an art of fighting with the body. It is the art of fighting with its habitual patterns.

THE MASTER'S VOICE

6

Inhale. Bend your back upwards and your head backwards. Keep your knees and hips off the floor.

7

Exhale. Raise your hips and bend the upper body inwards. Your heels remain pressed flat on the floor.

8

Inhale. Bring your other leg forward, bend your knee with your foot between your hands. Bend your back and look upwards.

THE MASTER'S VOICE

You touch the soul only when all the thoughts cease and you can feel your own presence.

9

Exhale. Bring the back leg beside your front foot, straighten your knees and bend your back down. Touch your palms to the floor and your forehead to your knees.

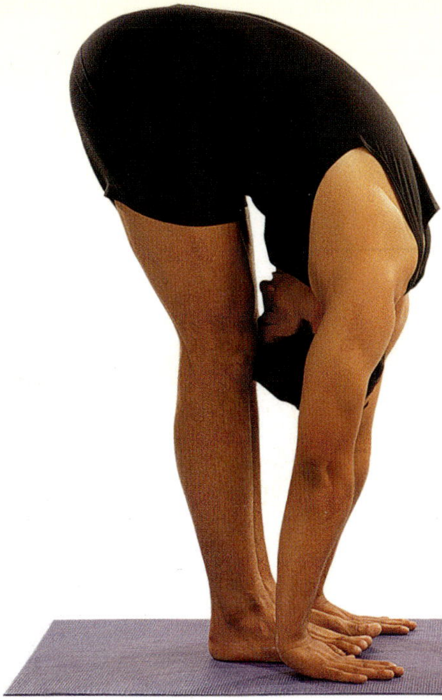

10

Inhale. Bring your upper body up and stretch your back and hands backwards. This completes one round. Practise five to ten rounds in the beginning and then gradually increase the number of rounds.

TADASANA

PALM TREE POSTURE

BENEFITS

Stretches the abdominal area and internal organs, improving digestion.

Stretches the back, shoulders, and neck muscles.

Stretches the quadriceps, calf muscles, and ankles.

1

Stand with your legs stretched apart. Stretch your arms outwards and come up on your toes.

The more intense the posture, the more easily you will slip into meditation.

THE MASTER'S VOICE

2

Inhale and take your hands up and join your palms. Stretch your whole body upwards. Hold the posture for 10-30 seconds.

VRIKSHASANA

TREE POSTURE

BENEFITS

Strengthens the muscles of the legs and knees.

Straightens the spine, helps digestion and presents stomach ailments.

Develops balance of body and mind, and enhances concentration.

CAUTION

People with weak knees should hold this posture for short durations and gradually increase the duration.

1

Stand straight with your legs together. Fold one leg and bring your foot close to your groin.

2

Maintain balance by focussing on a point in front of you. Straighten out your hands to your sides.

3

Raise your hands up, straighten them and join your palms. Hold the posture for 10-30 seconds. Then repeat with the other leg.

VEERASANA

WARRIOR'S POSTURE

BENEFITS

Strengthens the thighs, hamstrings, and calf muscles.

Stretches and opens up the groin and inner thighs.

Opens the chest and shoulders, and stretches and strengthens the back.

CAUTION

People with back pain and weak knees should avoid step 4.

Those with heart problems and high blood pressure should not practise this posture.

1

Stand straight with your legs wide apart and your hands on your hips.

2

Turn one leg and your upper body to one side and bend your knee.

3

Raise your hands up. Keep them straight and join your palms

4

Bend backwards as much as is comfortable. Stretch your stomach outwards and lower your hips. Hold the posture for 10-30 seconds. Then repeat on the other side.

BENEFITS

Stretches the sides and removes excess weight.

Tones and massages the internal organs of the abdominal area.

Increases the respiratory capacity of the lung.

CAUTION

Do not hold your breath while holding the posture.

ARDHACHAKRASANA

HALF-WHEEL POSTURE

1

Stand straight. Raise one hand to the side, keeping it straight.

2

Raise your hand up, beside your ear.

3

Gently bend your body to the side with your hand outstretched. Hold the posture for 10-30 seconds. Then repeat on the other side.

HASTAPADASANA

FORWARD BEND

BENEFITS

Massages and tones the abdomen.

Opens up the hips and stretches the hamstring muscles.

Increases blood flow to the head, improves metabolism, concentration, and vitality.

CAUTION

Those with high blood pressure or severe back problems should not perform this posture.

1

Stand with your feet together and back straight.

Don't force silence. Just wait for it to happen.

THE MASTER'S VOICE

2

Exhale and bend forward from the waist to touch your knees with your forehead, and rest your palms on the floor. Hold the posture for 10-30 seconds. Breathe normally.

STANDING BHUJANGASANA

STANDING COBRA POSTURE

BENEFITS

Strengthens the muscles of the legs and knees.

Straightens the spine, helps digestion and prevents stomach ailments.

Develops balance of body and mind, and enhances concentration.

1

Stand straight with your legs slightly apart and hands on your hips.

2

Slowly bend backwards.

3

Reach your maximum stretch and hold for as long as is comfortable. Keep your eyes open throughout. Repeat this three times.

TRIKONASANA

TRIANGLE POSTURE 1

BENEFITS

Stretches the hamstrings and calf muscles.

Tones the sides, causing loss of weight and the removal of what are called 'love handles'.

Massages the internal organs of the abdominal area.

Stretches the back, especially the sides of the back, and shoulders.

CAUTION

People with severe back conditions should not perform this posture.

1

Stand with your legs wide apart.

2

Bend one elbow and place your fingers in the armpit.

3

Slide the other hand along the leg and simultaneously bend the side of your body. Hold the posture for 10-30 seconds. Then repeat on the other side.

TRIKONASANA

TRIANGLE POSTURE 2

BENEFITS

Stretches the sides and removes excess weight.

Tones and massages the internal organs of the abdominal area.

Increases the respiratory capacity of the lung.

CAUTION

People with severe back conditions should not perform this posture.

1

Stand with your legs wide apart and your hands stretched out.

2

Bring your hand down towards the opposite ankle and raise your other hand backwards.

3

Hold your ankle and raise the other hand up. Turn your neck and look towards the upturned hand. Hold the posture for 10-30 seconds. Then repeat on the other side.

TRIKONASANA

TRIANGLE POSTURE 3

1

Stand with your legs wide apart. Turn one foot outwards and look in that direction.

2

Slide your hand down the leg by bending one side of the body.

3

Place your hand on the ankle and stretch the other hand straight, over and across your shoulders. Keep your upper shoulder pushed back slightly. Hold the posture for 10-30 seconds. Then repeat on the other side.

BENEFITS

Stretches the sides and removes excess weight.

Tones and massages the internal organs of the abdominal area.

Increases the respiratory capacity of the lung.

CAUTION

People with severe back conditions should not perform this posture.

PARSVAKONASANA

SIDE-SPLIT POSTURE

BENEFITS

Stretches the groin and hamstrings, and strengthens the quadriceps.

Massages the internal organs of the abdominal area, stimulating the digestive process.

Stretches the sides and removes excess weight around the stomach.

CAUTION

People with sciatica should avoid this posture.

1

Stand with your legs apart.

2

Turn one leg to the side, looking in that direction.

3

Lower your body to the side and lower the same hand as the bent knee to the floor.

4

Stretch the opposite hand outwards and look towards your fingertips. Hold the posture for 10-30 seconds. Then repeat on the other side.

PADMASANA

LOTUS POSTURE

BENEFITS

A workout for the entire body—the legs are held in a lock, the abdomen is drawn in, the shoulders are pulled back, and the back, arms, neck, and head are straightened. The whole body is toned by sitting in *padmasana*.

Allows the body to remain steady for long periods of time, which allows the mind to become calm—a requirement for meditation.

Stagnant blood is drained from the legs and directed towards the abdominal region, thus stimulating the digestive process.

1

Sit with your back straight and legs outstretched.

2

Fold one leg and place your ankle on the opposite thigh, close to the groin.

CAUTION

People suffering from sciatica, sacral infections, weak or injured knees should not perform this posture.

3

Fold your other leg and place it over the thigh of the bent leg, close to the groin. Sit with your back straight.

4

Perform *chin* mudra (see p. 115) with your hands. Hold the posture for as long as is comfortable. Practise alternatively with either leg on top.

BENEFITS

Develops the strength of the back by ensuring it is kept straight.

Improves digestion and alleviates ailments of the stomach such as constipation, hyperacidity and peptic ulcer.

Induces a state of stillness in the body that is a pre-requisite for meditation.

CAUTION

People with injured knees or ankles should avoid this posture.

VAJRASANA

THUNDERBOLT POSTURE

1

Sit with your legs stretched and your back straight.

2

Bend one knee and bring your ankle towards your buttocks. Place your foot under your buttock.

3

Fold your other leg and bring your ankle under your buttock. Place the toes of one foot on top of the other and sit on your feet. Keep your back straight and hold for as long as is comfortable.

SUKHASANA

EASY POSTURE

BENEFITS

Being one of the meditative postures, *sukhasana* calms the body and prepares the whole being for meditation.

Strengthens the back by ensuring that it is kept straight.

Retains the energy within the body for the purpose of meditation.

1

Sit with your legs stretched out. Bend one knee and draw your leg towards the groin. Place your foot in the back of the other knee.

2

Bend the other knee and draw your leg under your bent leg.

3

Flatten your knees and place your hands on them. Keep your back and head straight and your body relaxed. Hold for as long as is comfortable.

PASCHIMOTTANASANA

BACK-STRETCH POSTURE

BENEFITS

Stretches the muscles of the back and increases blood circulation to the spinal nerves.

Stretches and tones the hamstrings and calf muscles.

Presses the stomach area downwards, reducing fat and massaging the internal organs.

Used in yoga therapy for the management of kidney ailments, diabetes, colitis, and menstrual disorders.

CAUTION

People who suffer from slipped disc or sciatica should avoid this posture.

1

Sit with your back straight and legs stretched.

2

Inhale and raise your hands upwards.

3

Start exhaling and lower your back.

4

Hold your ankles and stretch your back, pulling your body downwards. Lower your forehead to the knees and bend your elbows to the floor. Breathe normally. Hold the posture for 10-30 seconds.

JANUSIRSASANA

HEAD-TO-KNEE POSTURE

BENEFITS

Stretches the hamstrings and flexes the hip joints.

Tones the internal organs of the abdominal area and helps lose excess weight.

Enhances stimulation of the nerves and muscles of the spine.

Used in yoga therapy for the management of diabetes, prolapse, menstrual disorders, colitis, and bronchitis.

CAUTION

Those with slipped disc or sciatica should avoid this posture.

1

Sit with your back straight and legs stretched.

2

Fold one leg and take your foot to the groin. Inhale, raise your hands up, keeping them straight.

3

Exhale, bend your back and lower your body, grasping the heel with your hands, bring your forehead down to touch your knee. Keep your other leg straight. Breathe normally. Hold for 10-30 seconds.

ARDHA MATSYENDRASANA

HALF-SPINAL-TWIST POSTURE

BENEFITS

Stretches the back in a spinal twist increasing flexibility of the back, toning spinal nerves, and relieving muscular back spasms.

Massages the abdominal organs, and alleviates digestive ailments.

Is used in yoga therapy for the management of diabetes since it squeezes the pancreas, forcing the secretion of insulin.

CAUTION

Pregnant women should avoid this posture after the second month.

People suffering from hernia, hyper-thyroidism and peptic ulcer should avoid this posture.

1

In a seated posture, place one leg (with the knee bent) across your other leg.

2

With the opposite hand lock your knee from outside and grasp your foot.

3

Fold your free hand behind your back and twist the spine to look back. Hold the posture for 10-30 seconds. Then repeat on the other side.

BENEFITS

By stretching the stomach and abdominal area it stimulates the digestive system and alleviates constipation.

Alleviates backache, drooping shoulders, and rounded back conditions.

Stretches the neck backwards thus regulating the functioning of the thyroid gland.

CAUTION

Those suffering from severe back conditions such as lumbago should seek expert advice before attempting this posture.

Those with enlarged thyroid should also seek expert guidance.

USHTRASANA

CAMEL POSTURE

1

Sit in *vajrasana* (see p. 44).

2

Come up onto your knees, bend backwards and drop your hands onto your ankles. Lower your head backwards.

3

Bend your back further down and stretch your hips out. Hold the posture for as long as is comfortable. Then release one hand at a time, straighten your back and return to *vajrasana*.

MARJARIASANA

CAT STRETCH POSTURE

1

Rest on your knees and hands, keeping your back straight.

2

Inhale. Bend your spine and raise your back and head upwards. Look up.

3

Exhale. Bend your spine and curve your back. Bend your head down and look at your navel. Repeat five times.

BENEFITS

Makes the back and neck supple and flexible.

Forces the body to bring focus and co-ordination between breath and movement.

Provides relief to women suffering from menstrual disorders and may be practised during menstruation for relief from cramps.

CAUTION

Those with severe backache should do this with care.

AKARNA DHANURASANA

CLOSE-TO-THE-EAR BOW POSTURE

BENEFITS

Stretches the back, shoulders, and hip muscles.

Massages the sides and internal organs of the abdomen.

Stretches the hamstrings.

CAUTION

This posture should be attempted after loosening up stretches.

People with severe back conditions and sciatica should avoid this posture.

Once you have known the body, you have known your breath and your mind. Then begins the journey to the unknown, where for the first time your ego merges with the superconscious.

THE MASTER'S VOICE

1

Sit with your legs stretched out. Bending your body forward, reach out and hold your big toes.

2

Fold one leg and draw your foot towards your chest.

3

Pull your foot as far from the other foot as possible. Hold the posture for 10-30 seconds. Then repeat with the other leg.

BENEFITS

Strengthens the arms, wrists, and shoulders.

Strengthens the back muscles, especially the lower back.

Strengthens the abdominal muscles.

CAUTION

People with high blood pressure and severe heart conditions should avoid this posture.

LOLASANA

SWINGING POSTURE

1

Sit in *padmasana* (see p. 42).

2

Place your hands straight, alongside your hips with the palms on the floor and fingers pointing forward.

3

Raise and balance your body off the floor. Swing the body backward and forward between the hands. Then return to the floor. Hold the posture for 10-30 seconds.

EK PAD ARDHAPADMASANA

ONE-LEGGED-HALF-LOTUS POSTURE

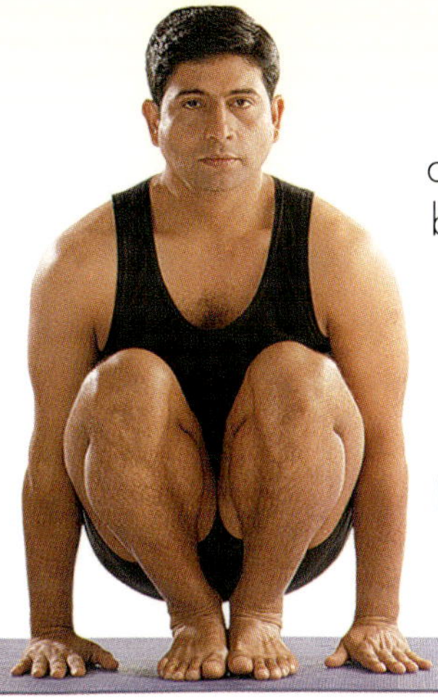

1

Sit on your haunches and support your body by placing your hands on the floor.

2

Lift one leg and place your ankle over the knee.

BENEFITS

Strengthens the legs, toes, and ankles.

Regulates the functioning of the reproductive system.

CAUTION

People with severe knee conditions and weak ankles should avoid this posture.

3

Focus on a point in front of you to maintain balance. Gradually raise your other hand and maintain balance. Perform namaste with your two palms joined.

MERU WAKRASANA

SPINAL TWIST

BENEFITS

This asana stretches the spine, loosens the vertebrae, and tones the spinal nerves.

Relieves sciatica, lumbago, and neck pain.

Prepares the back for more difficult asanas.

CAUTION

People with severe back conditions, ulcers, and hernia should avoid this posture.

1

Sit with your back straight and legs stretched out. Bend your right knee.

2

Place your right palm on the floor slightly behind the level of the hips.

3

Bring your left hand to the outer side of the right leg and place it on the floor beside your right ankle. Look over your right shoulder. Hold the posture for 10-30 seconds. Then repeat on the other side.

UTHAN PADASANA ARDHA HALASANA

RAISED-LEG-HALF-PLOUGH POSTURE

1

Lie flat on your back. Keeping your knees straight, raise your legs up.

2

Bring your legs perpendicular to the floor.

Gently raise your hips off the floor and raise your legs higher up. Hold the posture for as long as is comfortable. Return to the starting posture.

BENEFITS

Tones and strengthens the muscles of the abdomen.

Massages and exerts a pressure on the internal organs of the stomach area.

Strengthens the back and leg muscles.

CAUTION

People with severe back pain should avoid this posture.

VIPRIT KARNI ASANA

INVERTED POSTURE

BENEFITS

Redirects the flow of blood towards the brain, pituitary, and pineal glands, enhancing the mental faculties and alertness.

Strengthens the shoulders and back.

1

Lie flat on your back.

Drains stagnant blood from the legs and directs it towards the reproductive organs, relieving prolapse, hernia, and numerous sexual disorders.

Stimulates the appetite and relieves abdominal ailments like constipation.

2

Raise your legs up, stretching them straight.

CAUTION

Those suffering from high blood pressure, heart disease or enlarged thyroid should avoid this posture.

3

Raise your back off the floor and lower your legs towards your head.

4

Bring your legs perpendicular to the floor and support your hips with your hands. Keep your legs straight. Hold the posture for as long as is comfortable.

SARVANGASANA

SHOULDER STAND

1

Lie flat on your back.

2

Raise you legs up, stretching them straight.

3

Raise your back off the floor and lower your legs towards your head.

BENEFITS

Enriches blood flow to the face and brain.

Tranquilizes the mind. Relieves stress, fear, headaches, and psychological disturbances.

Boosts the immune system.

Encourages development of bones and regeneration of tissues.

Tones legs, abdomen, and reproductive organs.

Improves flexibility of the neck. Tones the nerves passing to the brain.

Revitalizes the ears, nose, throat, and eyes, boosting their immunity.

Regulates the functioning of the thyroid gland

4

Bring your legs perpendicular to the floor and support your hips with your hands. Keep your legs straight and stretched out.

5

Using your shoulders and your hands on your hips for support, gradually raise your legs higher. Slowly bring your hands lower down your back towards your shoulders and support the whole body from shoulders to feet in a straight line. Keep your chin pressed against the chest. Hold the posture for as long as is comfortable (not exceeding 2 minutes). Then gradually lower your back onto the floor and slowly bring your legs down without any strain or jerky movement to the back.

Very effective in the treatment of asthma, diabetes, colitis, menopausal and menstrual disorders.

CAUTION

Should be avoided by people suffering from enlarged thyroid, liver or spleen, cervical spondylitis, slipped disc, high blood pressure, heart ailments, weak blood vessels in the eyes, thrombosis.

Should be avoided during menstruation and advanced stages of pregnancy.

BENEFITS

Strengthens the muscles of the shoulders and neck and helps alleviate cervical spondylitis.

Regulates the functioning of the thyroid and thymus glands, and improves the immune system.

Alleviates abdominal ailments such as constipation.

CAUTION

Should be avoided by people suffering from ailments such as peptic ulcer, hernia, severe back conditions or any other illness.

Should not be practised during pregnancy.

MATSYASANA

FISH POSTURE

1

Sit in *padmasana* (see p. 42). Slowly lower your back to the floor. Fold your elbows and place the palms on the floor, fingers pointing towards your feet.

2

Using your arms, raise your head and shoulders. Turn your head downwards and rest on the crown of your head. Grasp your toes with your fingers. Hold the posture for 10-30 seconds.

3

Release your toes. Relax your head and raise your shoulders by propping them on your elbows. Straighten your elbows one at a time and raise yourself back to *padmasana*.

BENEFITS

Strengthens the muscles of the shoulders and neck and helps alleviate cervical spondylitis.

Improves the flexibility and circulation to the back.

Regulates the functioning of the thyroid and thymus glands, improving the immune system.

Alleviates abdominal ailments such as constipation.

CAUTION

Should not be practised by people suffering from arthritis of the neck, hernia, slipped disc, sciatica, high blood pressure, and severe back conditions.

HALASANA

PLOUGH POSTURE

1

Lie flat on your back. Raise your legs stretching them straight.

4

Fold your arms. Interlock your palms and place them behind your head.

2

Raise your back off the floor and bring your legs towards your head.

3

Gradually lower your legs and touch the floor with your toes. Straighten your knees.

5

If you are comfortable in this posture you can bend your knees and drop them to the floor. Take your hands over your legs and interlock them once again. Stay in this posture for as long as is comfortable. Do not over-strain (not exceeding 30 seconds).

NAUKASANA VARIATION 1

BOAT POSTURE

BENEFITS

Stretches the spine, enhancing blood circulation and tones of the spinal nerves.

Strengthens the abdominal muscles and removes excess fat around the stomach.

Massages the internal organs in the stomach area such as the kidneys and spleen.

Creates a mild stretch and tones the hamstrings.

CAUTION

People with neck and lower back problems should avoid this posture.

1

Lie flat on your back. Bend your knees and raise your legs. Fold your hands behind your head. Inhale.

2

Exhale and raise your head carefully.

3

Raise your head and shoulders to the maximum. Breathe normally. Hold the posture for 10-30 seconds. Then relax your muscles and return to the starting posture.

NAUKASANA VARIATION 2

BOAT POSTURE

1

Lie flat on your back. Raise your legs upwards, keeping your knees straight. Fold your hands behind your head. Inhale.

2

Exhale and raise your head above the ground.

3

Raise your head and shoulders to the maximum. Breathe normally. Hold the posture for 10-30 seconds. Then relax your muscles and return to the starting posture.

BENEFITS

Stretches the spine, enhancing blood circulation and tones of the spinal nerves.

Strengthens the abdominal muscles and removes excess fat around the stomach.

Massages the internal organs in the stomach area such as the kidneys and spleen.

Creates a mild stretch and tones the hamstrings.

CAUTION

People with neck and lower back problems should avoid this posture.

MERUDANDASANA

SPINAL COLUMN POSTURE

BENEFITS

Twists and stretches the spine, enhancing blood circulation and tones the spinal nerves.

Stretches the stomach muscles and improves digestion.

Massages the internal organs in the stomach area such as the kidneys and spleen.

Creates a mild stretch and tones the hamstrings.

1

Lie flat on your back.Stretch your arms out. Bend one knee and place it on the other knee.

CAUTION

People with severe back conditions should do this posture gently.

2

Gently twisting the spine, take your knee towards the floor. Look in the opposite direction.

3

Hold your knee to the floor. Hold the posture for 10-30 seconds. Then repeat on the other side.

MERUDANDASANA VARIATION 1

SPINAL COLUMN POSTURE

BENEFITS

Twists and stretches the spine, enhancing blood circulation and tones the spinal nerves.

Stretches the stomach muscles and improves digestion.

Massages the internal organs in the stomach area such as the kidneys and spleen.

Creates a mild stretch and tones the hamstrings.

CAUTION

People with severe back conditions should avoid this posture.

1

Stretch your arms outward. Raise one leg straight upwards. Place your heel on the toes of the other foot.

2

Gently twisting the spine, take your leg across your body and place it on the floor. Look in the opposite direction. Hold the posture for 10-30 seconds. Then repeat on the other side.

MERUDANDASANA VARIATION 2

SPINAL COLUMN POSTURE

1

Stretch your arms outward.
Fold your knees.

2

Gently twisting the spine, bend your legs sideways and place the knees on the floor. Look in the opposite direction. Hold the posture for 10-30 seconds. Then repeat on the other side.

BENEFITS

Twists and stretches the spine, enhancing blood circulation and tones the spinal nerves.

Stretches the stomach muscles and improves digestion.

Massages the internal organs in the stomach area such as the kidneys and spleen.

Creates a mild stretch and tones the hamstrings.

CAUTION

People with severe back conditions should avoid this posture.

MERUDANDASANA VARIATION 3

SPINAL COLUMN POSTURE

BENEFITS

Twists and stretches the spine, enhancing blood circulation and tones the spinal nerves.

Stretches the stomach muscles and improves digestion.

Massages the internal organs in the stomach area such as the kidneys and spleen.

Creates a mild stretch and tones the hamstrings.

1

Stretch your arms out. Fold your knees and place one foot on the other knee.

CAUTION

People with severe back conditions should avoid this posture.

2

Gently twisting your spine, bend your legs sideways towards the floor. Look in the opposite direction.

3

Hold your knees to the floor. Hold the posture for 10-30 seconds. Then repeat on the other side.

MERUDANDASANA VARIATION 4

SPINAL COLUMN POSTURE

BENEFITS

Twists and stretches the spine, enhancing blood circulation and tones the spinal nerves.

Stretches the stomach muscles and improves digestion.

Massages the internal organs in the stomach area such as the kidneys and spleen.

Creates a mild stretch and tones the hamstrings.

1

Stretch your arms out. Raise one leg up, keeping your knee straight.

CAUTION

People with severe back conditions should avoid this posture.

2

Gently twisting the spine, bring your leg across the body, and downwards towards the floor. Look in the opposite direction.

3

Place your leg on the floor. Keep your knee straight. Hold the posture for 10-30 seconds. Then repeat on the other side.

MERUDANDASANA VARIATION 5

SPINAL COLUMN POSTURE

BENEFITS

Twists and stretches the spine, enhancing blood circulation and tones the spinal nerves.

Stretches the stomach muscles and improves digestion.

Massages the internal organs in the stomach area such as the kidneys and spleen.

Creates a mild stretch and tones the hamstrings.

CAUTION

People with severe back conditions should avoid this posture.

1

Stretch your arms out. Raise your legs upwards, keeping the knees straight.

2

Gently twisting the spine, bring your legs down towards one side, keeping them together. Look in the opposite direction.

3

Place your legs on the floor. Keep your knees straight. Hold the posture for 10-30 seconds. Then repeat on the other side.

CHAKRASANA

WHEEL POSTURE

BENEFITS

Strengthens the shoulders which takes the weight of the body.

Strengthens the back and makes it flexible and supple.

Stretches the stomach and is beneficial to the digestive and respiratory systems.

Regulates the hormonal secretions of the body.

CAUTION

Should be avoided by people with weak wrists.

Should not be practised during any illness or pregnancy or when feeling tired.

1

Lie flat on your back with your legs folded and the feet on the floor, close to your buttocks.

3

Using your hands and thighs, gently raise your shoulders and head off the floor.

2

Fold your elbows and bring the palms beside your neck with the fingers pointing towards your shoulders.

4

Gradually raise your body by straightening your hands and legs and stretching your stomach outward. Curve your back completely and drop your head downwards. Hold the posture for 10-30 seconds. Then return to the starting point.

BENEFITS

Increases flexibility of the spine.

Increases blood circulation to the nerves in the spinal column and strengthens the spine.

Stretches the stomach area and is beneficial to the internal organs. Stimulates appetite.

Regulates the thyroid gland and alleviates menstrual disorders.

BHUJANGASANA

COBRA POSTURE

1

Lie flat on your stomach with your palms on the floor beside your shoulders. Rest your feet on your toes.

2

Inhale and raise your head, shoulders and upper back.

CAUTION

People with severe back and shoulder conditions should avoid doing step 3.

People suffering from peptic ulcer, hernia or hyper-thyroidism should avoid this posture.

3

Curve your back backward to its maximum stretch by straightening out your shoulders. Look upwards. Hold the posture for as long as you can hold your breath. Exhale and return to the floor. Repeat five times.

DHANURASANA

BOW POSTURE

BENEFITS

The spinal column is stretched, improving blood circulation to the spinal nerves.

The chest area is expanded increasing breathing capacity, hence helps in the treatment of asthma and other chest ailments.

1

Lie flat on your stomach.

Helps in the correction of hunching of the shoulders and spine.

CAUTION

Those suffering from a weak heart and high blood pressure should avoid this posture.

Those suffering from hernia, colitis, peptic or duodenal ulcers should avoid this.

3

Holding your ankles, begin to raise your legs and shoulders upwards.

2

Fold your knees and draw your feet down towards your buttocks.

4

Now stretch your legs upwards and raise your thighs off the floor. This creates a pull and raises your shoulders upwards. Look upwards. Hold the posture for 10-30 seconds.

BENEFITS

Strengthens the muscles of the back, especially the lower back.

Stimulates the autonomic nervous system.

Stimulates appetite and the digestive process, balances the functioning of the liver and other abdominal organs, and alleviates stomach disorders.

CAUTION

Should not be attempted by people with cardiovascular ailments and high blood pressure.

People suffering from peptic ulcer or hernia should avoid this posture.

PURNA SALABHASANA

LOCUST POSTURE

1

Lie flat on your stomach with your hands stretched forward. Relax your body.

2

Place your hands under your thighs, with palms touching the floor. Exhale. Raise your legs, keeping your knees straight. Keep your chin on the floor.

3

Raise your legs as high as possible. Hold the posture for 10-30 seconds. Then bring the legs back to the floor. Repeat three times.

ARDHA SALABHASANA VARIATION 1

HALF-LOCUST POSTURE

Lie flat on your stomach. Stretch your hands forward. Inhale and raise your right shoulder and left leg simultaneously. Keep the elbow and knee straight. Hold the posture for 10-30 seconds. Exhale and return to the floor. Repeat on the other side.

BENEFITS

Strengthens the arms and shoulders.

Strengthens the back muscles, especially the lower back.

Strengthens the abdominal muscles.

CAUTION

Those with enlarged thyroid should seek expert guidance.

ARDHA SALABHASANA VARIATION 2

HALF-LOCUST POSTURE

BENEFITS

Strengthens the muscles of the back, especially the lower back.

Stimulates the autonomic nervous system.

Stimulates appetite and the digestive process.

Balances the functioning of the liver and other abdominal organs, and alleviates stomach disorders.

CAUTION

People suffering from peptic ulcer or hernia should avoid this posture.

1

Lie flat on your stomach. Place your hands under your thighs with your palms touching the floor.

2

Exhale. Raise one leg upwards keeping your knee straight. Keep your chin on the floor. Hold the posture for 10-30 seconds. Then repeat with the other leg.

SIRSASANA

HEAD STAND

BENEFITS

Redirects the flow of blood towards the head, improving mental faculties like memory and concentration and reduces hair loss or dark circles under the eyes.

Relieves anxiety and other psychological and nervous disorders.

Drains stagnant blood from the legs and directs it towards the sexual organs. which stimulates the reproductive system and relaxes the legs.

1

Sit in *vajrasana* (see p. 44). Perform deep breathing.

2

Interlock your fingers and drop your hands to the floor. Ensure that your elbows touch your knees.

3

Gently place the crown of your head on the floor, locked against your palms.

4

Slowly raise your hips off the floor.

5

Gently raise your knees off the floor.

6

Straighten your knees.

7

Fold one leg and raise it.

8

Gradually with all the weight on your shoulders and head, raise the other leg.

9

Maintaining balance, slowly begin to raise the knees upwards. Practise this posture once you are comfortable balancing, then move ahead.

10

Slowly continue raising your knees upwards, without any strain.

11

Gradually straighten out your knees while maintaining balance. Do this in a relaxed manner, without any strain on your back or neck.

12

Hold the posture for as long as is comfortable (upto 1 minute). If you begin to fall backwards, quickly bend your back and roll on the floor.

CAUTION

Those suffering from high blood pressure and heart disease should not practise this posture.

Those suffering from severe eye ailments should avoid this posture.

Should be avoided during pregnancy and menstruation.

Should be avoided during a headache or migraine.

PADMA SIRSASANA

HEAD STAND IN LOTUS POSTURE

BENEFITS

The same as *sirasana* with the added benefit of toning the hamstrings.

CAUTION

Those suffering from high blood pressure and heart disease should not practise this posture.

Those suffering from severe eye ailments should avoid this.

Should be avoided during pregnancy and menstruation.

Should be avoided during a headache or migraine.

People with knee problems should avoid this posture.

1

Perform *sirsasana* (see p. 89). Then fold your legs without support into *padmasana*. Hold only for as long as is comfortable (not exceeding 1 minute)

2

Bend your legs downwards towards your chest.

3

Turn your hip to one side and hold the posture. Repeat on the other side. Release the legs, return to *sirsasana* and then bring your feet to the ground.

SHAVASANA

CORPSE POSTURE

BENEFITS

Relaxes the entire body and mind, removing physical and mental tiredness.

This is a good practice to help one fall asleep.

Develops awareness of the body and mind.

Lie flat on your back with your legs slightly apart and your hands loosely by your sides. Close your eyes and relax with your palms facing upwards. Practise deep abdominal breathing. This should be done at the end of your asana routine to relax the body.

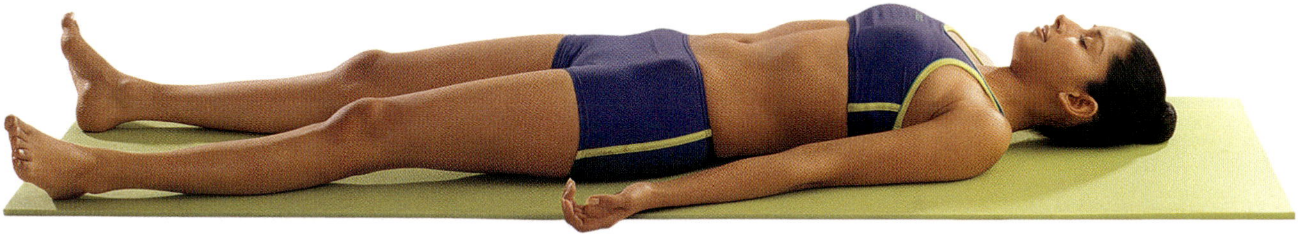

SUPTA SAHAJASANA

SLEEPING RELAXATION POSTURE

BENEFITS

This posture stimulates digestion and relieves constipation.

Relieves sciatic pain.

Redistributes excess weight around the waist.

Excellent relaxation position for people with backache and during advanced stages of pregnancy.

Lie down flat on your stomach, hands bent at the elbow, palms facing the ground, and shoulder joints relaxed.

Bend your leg at the hip and knee to get into a comfortable sleeping posture. Close your eyes and breathe normally.

MAKARASANA

CROCODILE POSTURE

BENEFITS

Strengthens the muscles of the back and is beneficial to tackle slipped disc, sciatica, and back pains.

Stretches the neck muscles and is useful for people with cervical spondylosis.

Increases the lung capacity, and is hence beneficial for asthmatics.

1

Lie flat on your stomach with the legs wide apart.

2

Fold one arm and bring it under your head.

3

Fold the other arm and bring it over the bent arm. Rest your head on your folded arms.

The mind is a phenomenon that results from the mental processes of creativity, analysis and memory. It is simply the read, heard and learnt chapters of life. The first sutra by one of the ancient masters of yoga, Patanjali, states, *ath yoganushasanam*—'now the discipline of yoga'. By 'now' Patanjali means the joy of no joy, the happiness of no happiness, the fun of no fun, the knowledge of no knowledge, the mind of no-mind. Beautifully explained as the beginning of no-mind, it means an understanding of calmness and silence, an understanding of the science of seeing and observing.

Following the mind cannot lead to happiness. With it, man can be manipulative, calculating and lastly, become more successful or unsuccessful. With no-mind, one walks in the valley of soundless sound. No-mind is nothing but the art of observing the doer—a pointer to the ultimate mixture of surrender, sincerity, and togetherness.

If the mind moves towards a meditative state, it enters a state of union. Any action taken in this state is right. That is why yoga talks about moving into that soundless sound which is emptying the mind. Yoga talks about meditation as a treatment for the unsettled mind. Strangely enough, when one meditates initially, is when one thinks the most. Don't think! Thoughtlessness is the gift of effort in the process of living in the right mind over a long period of time.

YOGA FOR THE MIND

KAPALABHATI KRIYA

FRONTAL BRAIN CLEANSING BREATH

BENEFITS

Increases the metabolic rate and reduces fat.

Improves the cardiorespiratory endurance and builds stamina.

Activates peristaltic movement in the stomach, resulting in better digestion and excretion.

Helps to cure sinus and migraine.

Revitalizes the system.

CAUTION

Those suffering from high blood pressure, gynaecological problems, stomach ailments or who have undergone recent surgery should consult their doctor before practising this posture.

Sit in *vajrasana* (see p. 44) or *padmasana* (see p. 42). Place your hands on your knees, with your back upright and eyes looking straight ahead. Exhale forcefully through your nose while pushing the stomach inward. Inhalation should be passive and short. Quickly perform the next exhalation. Do this continuously to a rhythm.

Practise this with fifty exhalations at a stretch, then increase to hundred. Subsequently, perform this for 2 minutes continuously and increase the duration to 10 minutes.

DHOKAN KRIYA

RESPIRATORY SYSTEM CLEANSING

Sit comfortably with your back and head straight. Place your hands on your knees. Start exhaling forcefully through your mouth, each time jerking the shoulders up and down. Do this to a rhythm.

Practise this with fifty exhalations at a stretch, then increase to hundred. Subsequently, perform this for 2 minutes continuously and increase the duration to 10 minutes.

BENEFITS

Forces out the residual toxic carbon dioxide from the lungs and increases the lung capacity.

Energizes the mind, removes sleepiness and prepares the mind for meditation.

Builds stamina.

CAUTION

Those suffering from high blood pressure, gynaecological problems, stomach ailments or who have undergone recent surgery should consult their doctor before practising this posture.

MOOLA BANDHA

ROOT LOCK

BENEFITS

Stimulates the urogenital and excretory systems and also intestinal peristalsis. Helps relieve ulcers, constipation, and piles.

Alleviates numerous sexual disorders, frustration and depression.

Beneficial for asthma, bronchitis, and arthritis.

CAUTION

Those with heart disease or high blood pressure, and pregnant women should avoid this posture.

1

Sit in *padmasana* (see p. 42). Place your hands on your knees.

2

Exhale completely and pull up the genital space and close the anal space. Keep your abdominal muscles tight. Do not inhale.

3

Then relax the lock and inhale. Repeat three times only.

UDYAAN BANDHA

ABDOMINAL LOCK

BENEFITS

Alleviates mild diabetes and many stomach ailments such as constipation, indigestion.

Abdominal organs are toned and massaged, and the blood circulation to the stomach area is enhanced.

Stimulates the solar plexus, influencing the distribution of energy.

CAUTION

Those with heart disease or high blood pressure, and pregnant women should avoid this posture.

1

Stand with your legs apart and slightly bent. Rest the palms on your thighs.

When you go deep into your mind you will find that it contains only thoughts and beliefs. Remove the contents and you have an empty container that is automatically filled with tremendous wisdom.

THE MASTER'S VOICE

2

Bend your back and exhale forcefully.

3

Now suck in your stomach.

4

Hold the contraction for as long as is comfortable to hold the breath. Then release the contraction and breathe in. Repeat only three times.

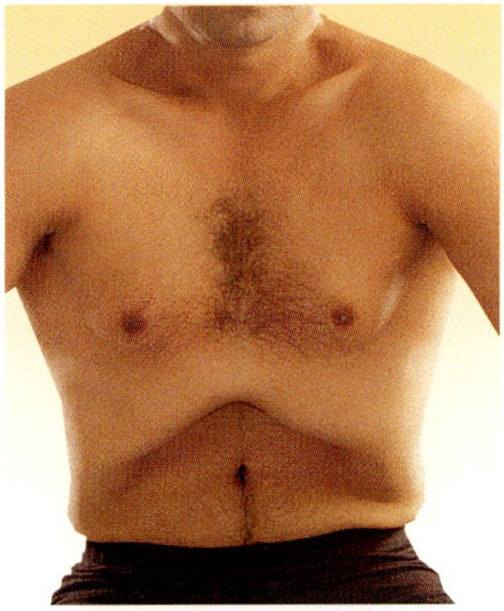

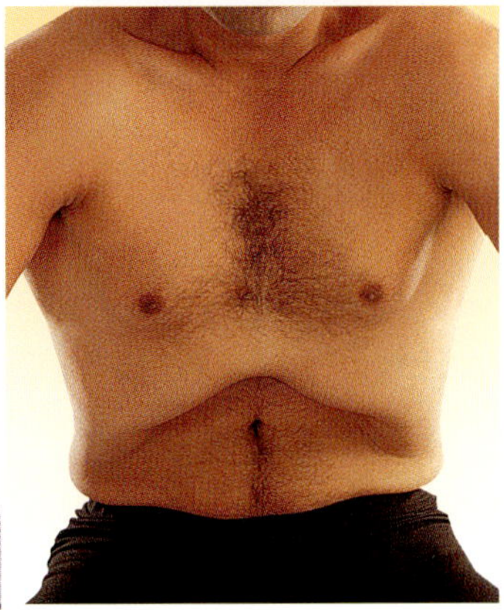

JALANDHAR BANDHA

THROAT LOCK

BENEFITS

Regulates the functioning of the thyroid gland and improves metabolism.

Causes decreased heart rate and increased breath retention.

Relieves stress, anxiety and anger, and helps to relax.

CAUTION

Those suffering from cervical spondylosis, high blood pressure, vertigo and heart disease should avoid this posture.

1

Sit in *padmasana* (see p. 42).

2

Inhale and lock your chin against your chest. Puff up the chest slightly and retain the breath inside for as long as is comfortable. Then release the chin lock, look up and exhale.

Repeat only three times.

MAHA BANDHA

GREAT LOCK

BENEFITS

Gives the benefits of all three *bandhas*.

Checks the ageing process.

Soothes anger.

CAUTION

Maha bandha should not be attempted until all the other three *bandhas* have been mastered.

1

Sit in *padmasana* (see p. 42). Exhale through the mouth forcefully and retain the breath outside.

2

Perform *jalandhar*, *udyaan*, and *moola bandhas* successively in this order. Hold for as long as is comfortable. Release *moola*, *udyaan*, and *jalandhar bandhas* in this order. Inhale. Repeat only three times.

BENEFITS

Calms and stills the mind.

The vibrations caused by the humming sound that is produced has a soothing effect on the brain, and relieves stress, anxiety, insomnia, and high blood pressure.

Improves the voice.

CAUTION

This should not be performed while lying down.

Those with an ear infection should perform this after the infection has cleared up.

BHRAMARI PRANAYAMA

HUMMING BEE BREATHING

1

Sit in *vajrasana* (see p. 44). Close your eyes and relax.

2

Gently insert your thumbs in your ears and place the fingers comfortably on your head. Keep your mouth closed. Inhale. Exhale slowly through your mouth, (through the small gap between your teeth) making a rumbling sound by vibrating the lips. Ensure that the exhalation is happening through the mouth and not the nose.

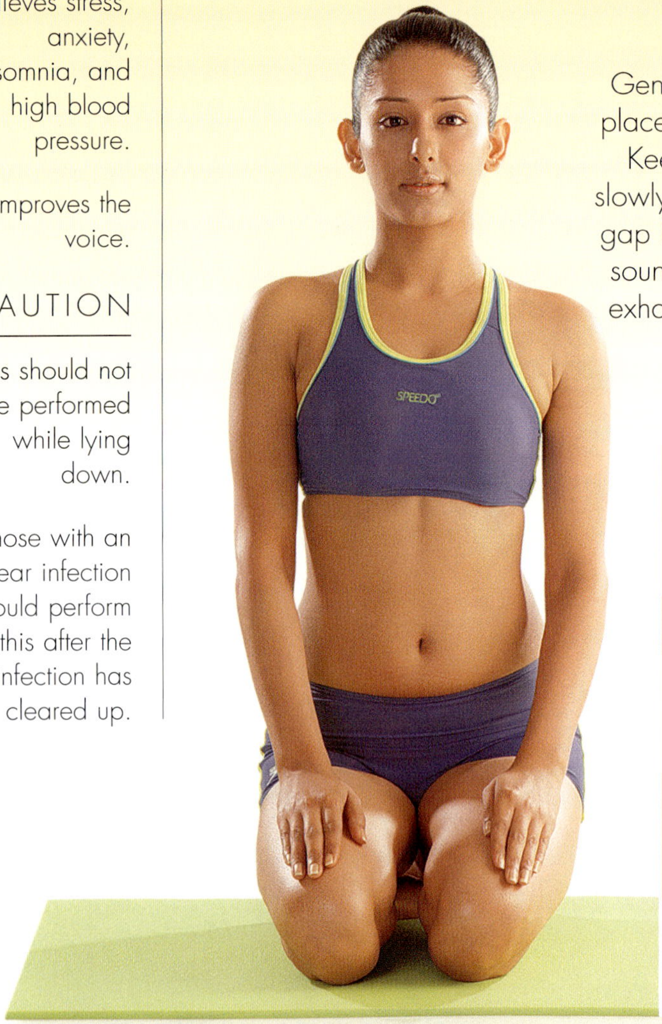

SHEETKARI PRANAYAMA

SQUARE LIP BREATHING

1

Sit comfortably with your back straight.

2

Open your lips to expose your teeth. Inhale through your mouth with your teeth loosely closed.

3

Exhale slowly through your nose. Repeat this procedure for 2-5 minutes. Ensure that your body does not get too cold.

BENEFITS

The cool, inhaled air aids in secreting stress-relieving hormones in the brain.

Cools the body, mind, and reduces mental excitement and is beneficial in bringing about sleep.

The gums and teeth are kept healthy.

CAUTION

Those with low blood pressure and respiratory illness should avoid this posture.

SHEETALI PRANAYAMA

ROLLED TONGUE BREATHING

BENEFITS

Cools the body by lowering the temperature.

Reduces anxiety and stress.

CAUTION

Those with low blood pressure and respiratory illness should avoid this posture.

1

Sit in *padmasana* (see p. 42) or *sukhasana* (see p. 45) with your back straight. Roll your tongue as shown.

2

Slowly inhale through the passage made by your tongue, to a count of five. Press your chin down on your neck. Hold your breath to a count of ten. Raise your chin, exhale through the nostrils to a count of ten. Repeat at least fifteen times. This can be done for an hour. If you feel very cold, stop immediately.

YOGA NIDRA

AWARENESS SLEEP

Lie on your back on a hard mattress. Wear minimal clothes. Concentrate on your breath. Inhale and exhale a few times. Breathe deeply from the abdomen. Do this about three times.

There are sixteen vital points in your body which can relax you totally if you concentrate on them. These points are the toes, ankles, calves, knees, thighs, abdomen, chest, shoulders, elbows, wrists, fingertips, neck, chin, lips, nostrils, and the forehead. Start the cycle of concentration from the forehead and move progressively to your toes and reverse this cycle, going back to your forehead. Repeat this cycle two to three times.

Now imagine your limbs are detached from your body, Only the head, chest, and the abdominal area exist now. As you breathe, feel the air entering your spine and cleansing it.

Now concentrate on the different vital nerve plexus or nerve junctions called chakras. Start from *mooldhara*, or the root plexus, which lies in the space between your anus and your genitals. Move to *swadhisthan*, four fingers above the navel, *anahat*, the midpoint of the chest, to *visudhi*, the throat, *ajna*, the point between the eyebrows, and finally, the *suryachakra* at the crown, the midpoint of the skull. Breathe in and out about ten times while concentrating on each chakra.

Imagine your limbs are once again attached to your body. Be aware of your whole body as one unit, for 2 minutes.

Slowly open your eyes and get up.

BENEFITS

Cures insomnia.

One of the most potent forms of stress-relief.

CAUTION

Avoid sleep while doing this.

NAULI KRIYA

ABDOMINAL MASSAGING

BENEFITS

Tones up and causes weight loss in the stomach area.

Induces appetite, intestinal peristalsis and proper digestion.

Alleviates ailments of the digestive system, including constipation and acidity.

CAUTION

To be practised 5-6 hours after eating, preferably in the morning.

1

Stand with your feet apart. Take in a deep breath and exhale through your mouth, emptying your lungs. Bend your knees slightly. Rest your hands on your thighs.

2

Madhyama Nauli (central abdominal contraction) Draw in the muscles of your lower abdomen.

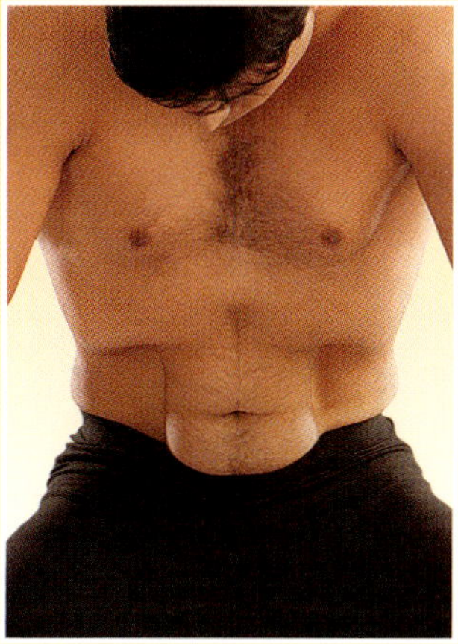

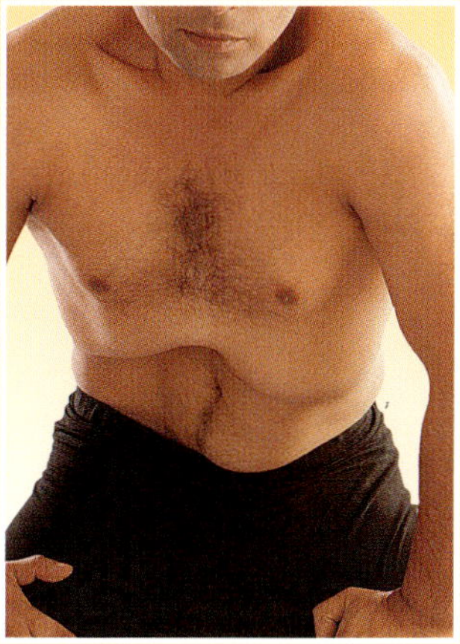

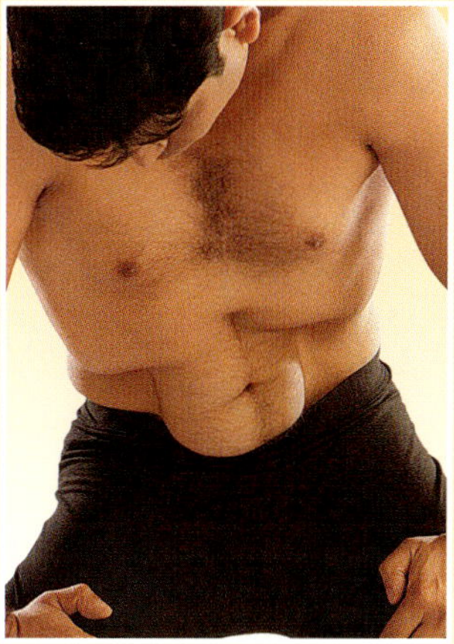

3

Contract your abdominal muscles and hold for as long as it is comfortable. Then release the muscles, stand upright and inhale. Repeat five times.

4

Vama Nauli
(left contraction)
Perform *madhyama nauli.* Isolate and strongly contract your abdominal muscles of the left side. Return to *madhyama nauli.* Then release the muscles, stand upright and inhale. Repeat five times.

5

Dakshina Nauli
(right contraction)
Perform *madhyama nauli.* Isolate and strongly contract your abdominal muscles of the right side. Return to *madhyama nauli.* Then release the muscles, stand upright and inhale. Repeat five times.

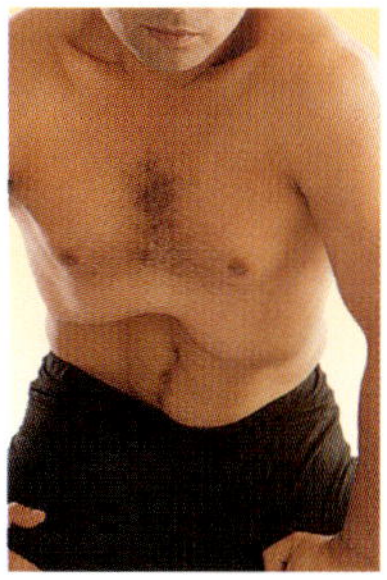

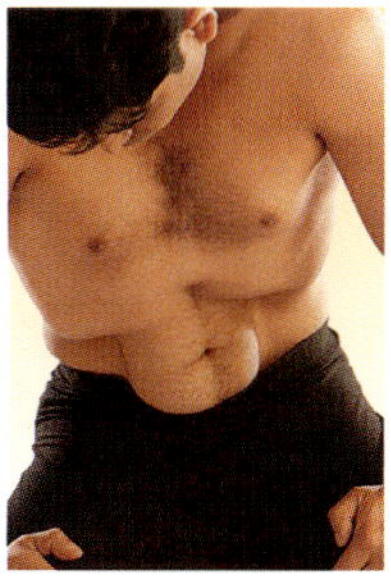

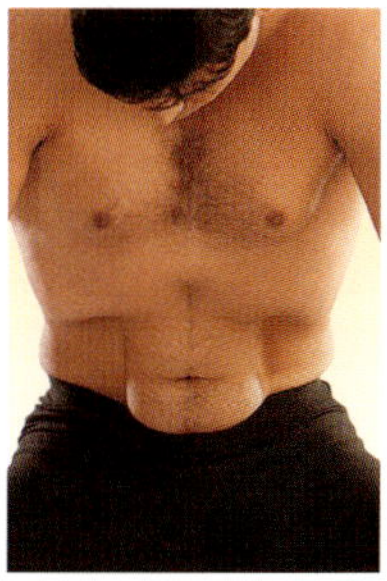

ABDOMINAL ROTATION

Contract the muscles to the left, then rotate to the right. Practise thrice. Then repeat from right to left. Finally contract the muscles in the centre. Relax the muscles and stand upright and breathe in.

The ancient yogi Patanjali, observed that for man to make progress on his chosen path he should practise asanas, pranayama, *kriyas*, *bandhas*, and mudras to awaken in him the subtle presence of the Almighty. He should then progress, over time, towards emptying his mind, and thus opening it up.

Yoga is a series of steps taken towards awakening the body, breath, mind, consciousness, intelligence, patience, and watchful awareness leading to the knowledge of the superior-conscious.

In order to reach a state of empty mind, Patanjali asks one to exercise the body, emotions, and mind, which will lead to a state of void that is blissful. His technique is like a mother putting her child to sleep. She murmurs a single line again and again. The child holds the mother's hand, enters a world created by her and is slowly lulled into a state of hypnosis. He lets go of himself and falls into a deep sleep thinking his mother is there, holding his hand. But the moment the child is asleep, she removes her hand from his grip, covers him with a blanket and leaves the room.

The process of awakening from one's sleep slowly, just like the mother's chant lulls into sleep, is the path of yoga. It allows one to be eased into awakening. On the path of yoga, one does not know how from the body one reaches the mind, and how from the mind one reaches a state of no-mind.

This is the path of yoga. It is difficult for man to take stock of his intelligence and ego. So Patanjali gives the security jacket of a process and then awakens you from your sleep.

YOGA FOR THE SOUL

SHARNAGAT MUDRA

GESTURE OF SURRENDER

BENEFITS

Stimulates the digestive process and massages the internal organs in the abdominal area.

Stretches the back muscles.

Relaxes the body and induces a state of inner withdrawal.

1

Sit in *vajrasana* (see p. 44). Stretch your hands forward and lower your back.

2

Lower your back and drop your head onto the floor, and slide the hands completely forward. Hold the posture for as long as is comfortable.

CHIN MUDRA

PSYCHIC GESTURE OF CONSCIOUSNESS

BENEFITS

Re-directs the flow of energy, that is usually lost at the fingertips. Thus ensures that energy in conserved for the purpose of meditation.

Sit in *padmasana* (see p. 42). Place your hands on your knees with the palms facing upwards. Place the tip of your forefinger on the centre of your thumb.

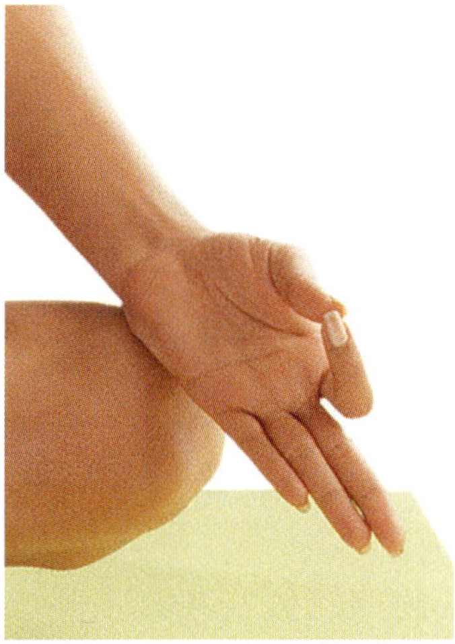

BENEFITS

Keeps the back straight in preparation for meditation.

The placement of the palms on top of each other induces a state of deep tranquility, in preparation for meditation.

SAHAJ MUDRA

SIMPLE MEDITATIVE GESTURE

1

Sit comfortably with your back and head straight. Close your eyes and relax. Breathe deeply.

You are not the body. You are not the mind. You are not the soul. To know who you are, you have to first know what you are not.

THE MASTER'S VOICE

2

Place your hands on your lap with the palms one on top of the other.

SHANMUKHI MUDRA

CLOSING THE SEVEN GATES

BENEFITS

This gesture of inner focusing balances the internal and external awareness and induces the state of *pratyahar* or sense withdrawal.

CAUTION

People suffering from depression should avoid this practice.

1

Sit in *padmasana* (see p. 42) and close your eyes. Relax. Close your ears with your thumbs.

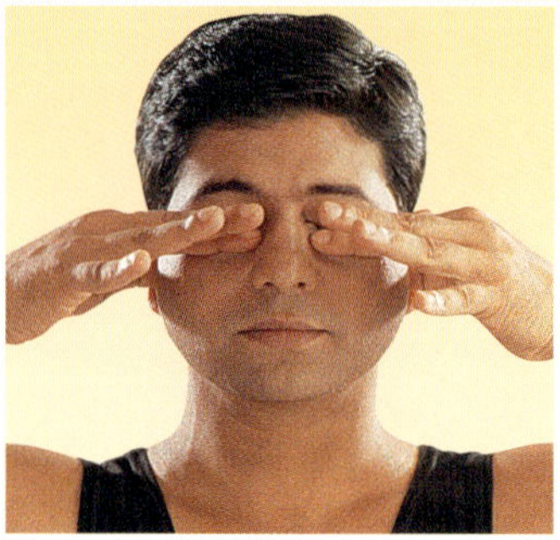

2

Close your eyes with your index fingers.

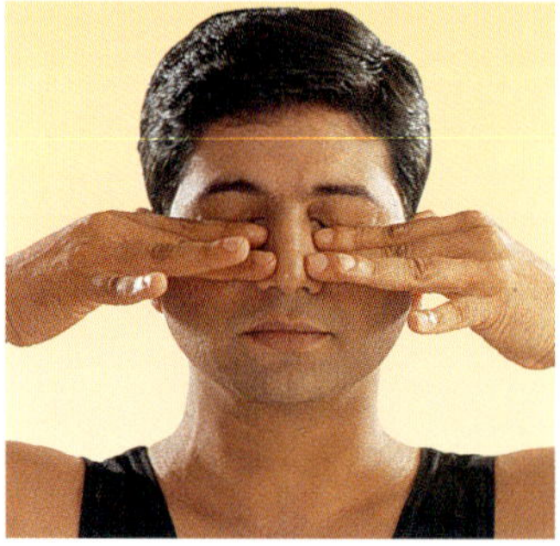

3

Close your nose with your middle fingers.

4

Close your mouth by placing your ring fingers above and the little fingers below your mouth.

When you realize you are not the body, not the mind, not even the soul, you open up to the silence inside you where you lose yourself to find eternal bliss.

THE MASTER'S VOICE

5

Release the pressure on the nostrils and take a deep breath. Close your nostrils and retain the breath inside. Now just listen to the sounds you hear within. Then release your hands. Keep practising till you begin to hear more subtle sounds.

BENEFITS

Stimulates the flow of energy through the different vital centres of the *pranic* body.

CHAKRAN BHEDAN DHYAN

NERVE PLEXUS AWARENESS PRACTICE

1

Sit in *padmasana* (see p. 42). Practise deep breathing throughout. Bring the awareness to the *mooladhara chakra*, at the perineum in the male body or at the cervix in the female body.

2

Bring the awareness to the *swadhisthana* chakra, situated in the spine directly behind the genital organs.

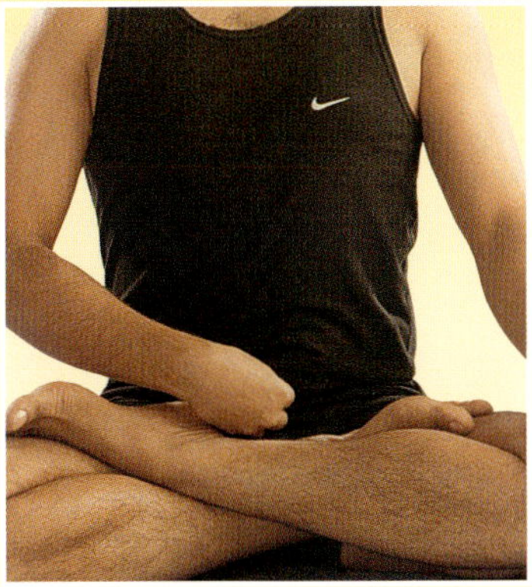

3

Bring the awareness to the *manipura* chakra, situated in the spine behind the navel.

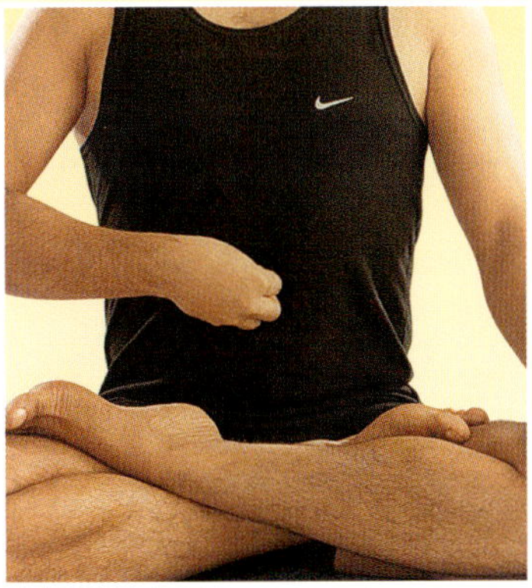

4

Bring the awareness to the *anahata* chakra, situated in the spine behind the sternum and level with the heart.

5

Bring the awareness to the *vishuddhi* chakra, situated at the back of the neck, behind the throat pit.

6

Bring the awareness to the *ajna* chakra, situated behind the centre of the eye-brows, in the mid-brain, at the top of the spine.

7

Bring the awareness to the *bindu* chakra, situated at the top, back portion of the head.

NASIKAGRADRISHTI

NOSE TIP GAZING

BENEFITS

Develops powers of concentration.

An excellent technique for calming anger.

Makes the eyes clear and bright.

Relieves tension, anxiety, depression, and insomnia.

CAUTION

Those suffering from glaucoma, diabetic retinopathy or those who have had cataract surgery, lens implants or other eye operation should not perform this exercise.

1

Sit in any meditative posture with your head and spine straight in *chin* mudra. Close your eyes and relax your whole body.

2

Open your eyes and focus on the tip of your nose without straining. When your eyes are correctly focused, the nose is seen as a V. Concentrate on the tip of the V. Become completely absorbed in this.

After a few seconds, close your eyes and relax them. Repeat for upto 5 minutes. Then practise palming (rub your palms together and then apply the warmth to your eyes).

ANHAD NAD

COSMIC SOUND / THE UNSTRUCK SOUND

BENEFITS

Takes you to the threshold of meditation.

1

Sit in *padmasana* (see p. 42). Place the *anhad* stand between your legs and groin.

2

Prop your elbows on the *anhad* stand and keep your back straight. Close your ears with your thumbs and place your fingers comfortably on your head.

3

Sit in silent meditation with complete awareness for as long as is possible and try to increase the duration every day.

BENEFITS

Is a powerful meditation technique.

Blocks the constant barrage of thoughts that besiege the mind at any given moment.

Relaxes and de-stresses the whole being.

SUMIRAN

CHANTING HIS NAME

1

Sit in a meditative posture (*padmasana, vajrasana, sukhasana*) and assume *chin* mudra with one hand and hold the *sumiran* mala in the other.

THE MASTER'S VOICE

Inner silence and peace is our natural state. But to reach that we have to destroy the beliefs, ideas and concepts which we have been accumulating since we were born.

2

Chant *'so-hum'* aloud as you pass each bead between your fingers.

BENEFITS

Improves flexibility by about 60 per cent. By yourself, you would be able to stretch to a certain level. Assisted by your partner, you would be stretched to your maximum, which you would be unable to do on your own.

Internal organs are massaged and many of the systems are brought to their maximum efficiency.

The body is toned and consequently weight is lost.

The internal hormonal benefits are the same as are associated with the respective poses.

Yoga is a science of togetherness, of the soul with the Almighty. Having a partner with who to do yoga is like performing in front of a mirror to view the intricacies of your own posture. Though historically, information on yoga for couples has been minimal, it holds importance because it can greatly increase a person's mobility and flexibility. It can make one more relaxed and sensitive, making one confident and prepared to perform otherwise difficult postures.

The human body is plastic and not elastic, meaning that once stretched to a certain point, the mobility of that joint or muscle increases and remains that way. It can help a yoga enthusiast to enter the art of yoga smoothly and painlessly. These partner stretches are a boon to those who are unfamiliar with yoga and who feel that they are unable to practise the postures described in the earlier chapters of this book.

Muscles stretch to about 35 per cent of their total intensity in a solo posture, but with added external pressure, the intensity and range of the posture increases up to 95 per cent. This additional pressure activates the glands better, and increases the flexibility and mobility of muscles. In addition, while a solo posture stretches some of muscles leaving others in a mild state of contraction, postures practised with a partner stretches them further because the person's body is completely relaxed and loose, in the hands of another.

So enjoy these unique stretches which will make your body supple and flexible in no time.

YOGA FOR

COUPLES

BENEFITS

Provides relief and relaxation from backache.

Stretches and opens the groin.

PARTNER STRETCH 1

1

Fold your partner's knee and push it towards her chest while keeping the other thigh pressed down. Hold till your partner feels a good stretch. Repeat with the other leg. Ask her to exhale continuously.

2

Now push her knee outwards while keeping the other thigh pressed down. Hold till your partner feels a good stretch. Repeat with the other leg. Ask her to exhale continuously.

PARTNER STRETCH 2

BENEFITS

Relieves pain in the back and provides relaxation.

Removes excess gas from the stomach and intestines.

CAUTION

Tell your partner to breathe normally as holding the breath will create unwanted pressure in the chest area.

Your partner lies flat on her back. Raise her legs and bend her knees towards her chest. Ask her to exhale continuously. Apply even pressure. Hold for as long as is comfortable.

PARTNER STRETCH 3

BENEFITS

Stretches the hamstrings.

Stretches the spine and lower back and provides relief and relaxation.

CAUTION

Make sure there is no strain on the knee if your partner's hamstrings are stiff.

Your partner lies flat on her back with hands stretched to her sides. You kneel by her side. Bend your partner's leg with her foot resting on the opposite knee. Holding her shoulder down, push the knee across the body towards the floor. The partner faces in the opposite direction. Hold till your partner feels a good stretch. Repeat with the other leg.

PARTNER STRETCH 4

Your partner lies flat on her back with hands stretched to her sides. Stand by her side. Raise your partner's leg and take it to the opposite side, across her body. Place your foot under the thigh of her straight leg. Place the calf of your partner's other leg against the shin of your other leg and straighten her knee. The partner faces in the opposite direction. Now walk your leg to the front till the partner's leg cannot go any further. Hold till your partner feels a good stretch. Repeat on the other leg.

BENEFITS

Stretches the hamstrings.

Stretches the spine and lower back, and provides relief and relaxation.

CAUTION

Make sure there is no strain on the knee if your partner's hamstrings are stiff.

BENEFITS

Stretches the hamstrings and calf muscles.

CAUTION

Avoid pressing the thigh too hard, as it may exert too much pressure on the knee.

PARTNER STRETCH 5

1

Your partner lies flat on the floor. Kneel down beside her. Your partner raises one leg and places the heel against your shoulder. Holding her toes with one hand, gently straighten her leg by applying pressure against her thigh. Hold till your partner feels a good stretch. Repeat with the other leg.

An asana is like a song. You can sing alone or sing a duet. What matters most is hitting the right note or perfecting the stretch.

THE MASTER'S VOICE

2

Your partner raises both her legs straight and places her heels against your chest. Stretch her toes downwards. Hold till your partner feels a good stretch.

BENEFITS

Applies pressure and strengthens the lower back, relieving backache.

Stretches the thighs and ankles.

CAUTION

If the knees don't bend fully, don't force the feet down beyond its limit.

PARTNER STRETCH 6

1

Your partner lies flat on her stomach. Fold her legs and hold her toes. Join the feet and push them gently against her buttocks. Hold till your partner feels a good stretch.

2

Separate her legs and push her feet gently downwards beside her buttocks. Hold till your partner feels a good stretch.

PARTNER STRETCH 7

Your partner lies flat on her stomach. Stand by her side. Lift one leg and hold her ankle. Place your foot gently at the base of her spine. Without exerting pressure with your foot, gently raise the ankle upwards. Hold till your partner feels a good stretch. Repeat with the other leg.

BENEFITS

Stretches and strengthens the lower back.

CAUTION

Do not place your weight on the back. Make sure the heel is not on the spine.

PARTNER STRETCH 8

BENEFITS

Stretches, strengthens, and alleviates pain in the muscles of the back.

CAUTION

Do not stretch too fast and be careful not to over-stretch.

Your partner lies flat on her stomach. Stand with your legs beside her hips. Hold your partner just above the elbows and stretch her shoulders upwards and towards you. Avoid straining your own back. Hold till your partner feels a good stretch.

PARTNER STRETCH 9

BENEFITS

Stretches and massages the back and provides immense relief and relaxation from backache.

Stretches the shoulders and removes any weariness from the shoulders.

CAUTION

Avoid pulling the hands too hard as you are mainly working with your legs.

Sit behind your partner. Hold her wrists and place your feet against her back. Straighten your knees and push her back inwards. She drops her head backwards. Hold till your partner feels a good stretch.

BENEFITS

Stretches the hamstrings, arms, and back.

CAUTION

To be avoided by people with spondylitis or high blood pressure.

PARTNER STRETCH 10

Your partner stands in front of you and you sit behind. Place your legs on her buttocks with your knees folded. Your partner bends down and passes her hands between her legs. Hold her hands tightly. Slowly start applying pressure by straightening your legs and gently pulling her hands. Hold till your partner feels a good stretch.

PARTNER STRETCH 11

BENEFITS

Stretches the lower back.

Stretches the stomach and massages the internal organs.

CAUTION

Support the lower back well and hold some of her weight, so that she is relaxed in her back bend.

Your partner stands straight with her legs apart. Stand in front and place one leg between her legs. Interlock your hands behind her lower back. She holds your shoulders and stretches her back and head backwards. Hold till your partner feels a good stretch.

PARTNER STRETCH 12

BENEFITS

Stretches and tones the sides of the body, and removes excess weight around the waist.

CAUTION

Make sure you are providing adequate support at her waist.

Your partner stands with her legs slightly apart. Stand by her side. She raises one hand straight upwards. Place your hand at her waist and with the other hand exert pressure above the elbow of her straight hand, bending her body to the side, away from you. Hold till your partner feels a good stretch. Repeat on the other side.

PARTNER STRETCH 13

Your partner sits with one leg folded and the other leg over the folded leg. Sitting at a slight angle in front, place one leg slightly bent on her knee and the other leg straight on her opposite shoulder. Your partner's head is turned over the shoulder and that hand is bent and placed behind her back. Hold her free hand with both your hands and stretch it. Hold till your partner feels a good stretch. Repeat on the other side.

BENEFITS

Stretches the hamstrings and outer thighs.

Twists the spine and relieves back pain, and stretches the shoulders.

CAUTION

Do this stretch slowly and be careful when to stop, as in this position, there is pressure on the lungs.

Avoid pulling the hand too much.

BENEFITS

Stretches and tones the entire side of the body, and removes excess weight from the sides.

Stretches and opens up the shoulders.

CAUTION

If your partner has sciatica, he/she should avoid this stretch.

PARTNER STRETCH 14

1

Your partner stands with her legs wide apart. Place one leg on her thigh and the other on her hip. The partner bends and you hold her fingers. Now gently stretch her hands towards you while keeping your legs fixed. Hold till your partner feels a good stretch. Repeat on the other side.

2

Interchange the position of the feet and stretch your partner further towards yourself. Hold till your partner feels a good stretch. Repeat on the other side.

PARTNER STRETCH 15

BENEFITS

Stretches the hamstrings and calf muscles.

Stretches the back.

CAUTION

If your partner has cervical spondylosis, he/she should avoid this stretch

Both you and your partner sit facing one another with your knees bent and feet against each other. Both bend forward and hold each other's hands. Now both exhale and slowly start straightening your knees; hold for as long as is comfortable.

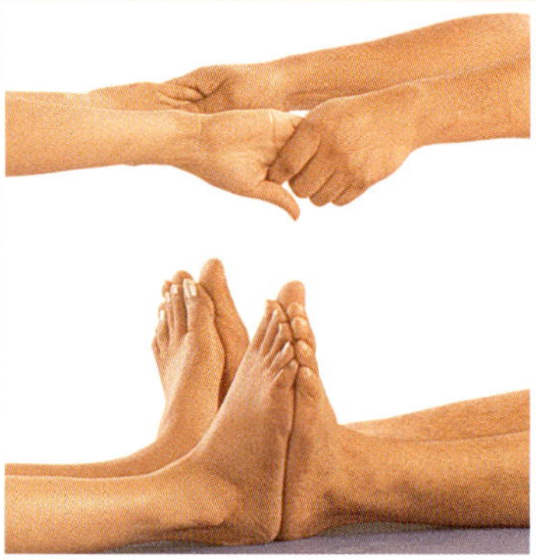

PARTNER STRETCH 16

BENEFITS

Stretches the groin and inner thighs.

Stretches the back.

CAUTION

If your partner has cervical spondylosis, he/she should avoid this stretch.

Both you and your partner sit with your legs stretched apart and heels against each other. Hold each other's hands. Gradually pull her towards yourself and hold. Ask your partner to breathe out. Hold till your partner feels a good stretch. Repeat two times.

BENEFITS

Stretches the groin.

Stretches the back.

CAUTION

If your partner has cervical spondylosis, he/she should avoid this stretch

PARTNER STRETCH 17

Your partner folds her legs, joins her feet and places them close to her groin. Place your feet against her shins and hold each other's hands. Gradually pull her towards yourself. Ask your partner to breathe out. Hold till your partner feels a good stretch. Repeat two times.

PARTNER STRETCH 18

Make your partner stand straight in front of you. Sit behind. Place your feet on the partner's buttocks. The partner bends her back and drops her hands. Hold her hands above the elbows. Now straighten your legs and let your partner drop herself slowly towards you. Lift your partner off the floor with your feet and hold her there. To bring her down, bend your knees and lower her towards your body. Then she can stand up. Hold only for as long as is comfortable for both of you.

BENEFITS

Stretches the whole body, especially the back and provides relief from backache.

CAUTION

People with severe back conditions, high blood pressure, and other heart conditions should not do this stretch.

To be avoided during pregnancy and menstruation.

Not to be given to overweight people.

In the nine months of pregnancy, an expectant mother forms a close bond with the child in her womb.

Yoga is the art of making this time of bonding relaxed and enjoyable. It is only yoga that works for the pregnant mother since she cannot do much after 6 months—asanas to relax the body, meditation to cleanse the mind, *bandhas* to secrete the right hormones and increase strength.

If practised with care, yoga can help the woman increase her will power which will aid in shedding habits like smoking and drinking. Chanting, relaxation and breathing exercises can do wonders in helping a woman through the pain of childbirth, making the whole process effortless. At a physical level, asanas help the vaginal wall to stretch to the size of the child's head. The practice of *bandhas* also brings the vaginal wall back into the right shape very quickly.

The ancients also researched the role of the external environment and the internal state of the mother on her offspring. If the mother is in harmony with herself—body, mind, and soul—this harmony will be relayed to her child.

YOGA FOR

PREGNANT

WOMEN

PAWANAMUKTASANA

NECK ROTATION

BENEFITS

Loosens up the muscles of the neck and the spinal nerves.

Relieves stress and exhaustion.

CAUTION

Avoid bending forward too much if you have cervical spondylitis.

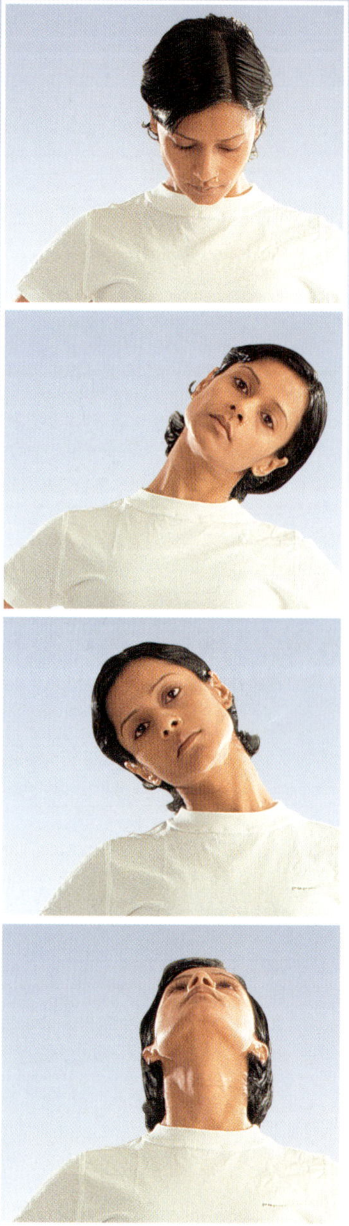

1

Stand straight and place your hands on your hips.

2

Rotate your neck in a complete circle a few times. Then repeat in the other direction.

PAWANAMUKTASANA

SHOULDER ROTATION

BENEFITS

Loosens up the muscles of the shoulders and back.

Relieves stress and exhaustion.

1

Stand straight. Fold your arms and place your fingers on your shoulders.

2

Rotate your shoulders completely a few times. Then repeat in the other direction.

BENEFITS

Loosens up the wrists.

Relieves stress and exhaustion.

PAWANAMUKTASANA

WRIST ROTATION

1

Stand straight and raise your hands forwards. Clench your fists.

2

Rotate your fists ten times in the clockwise and then counter-clockwise direction.

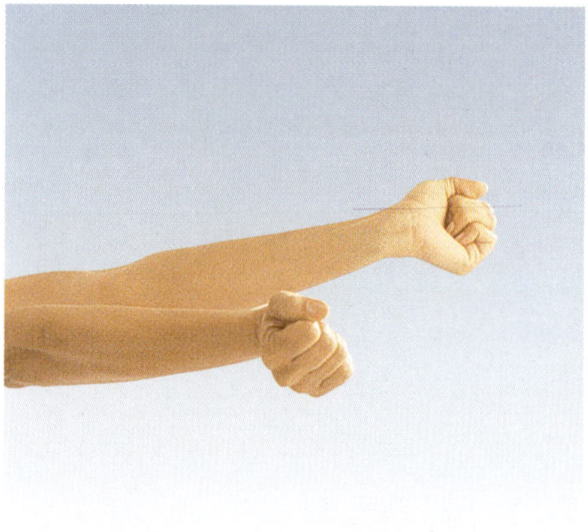

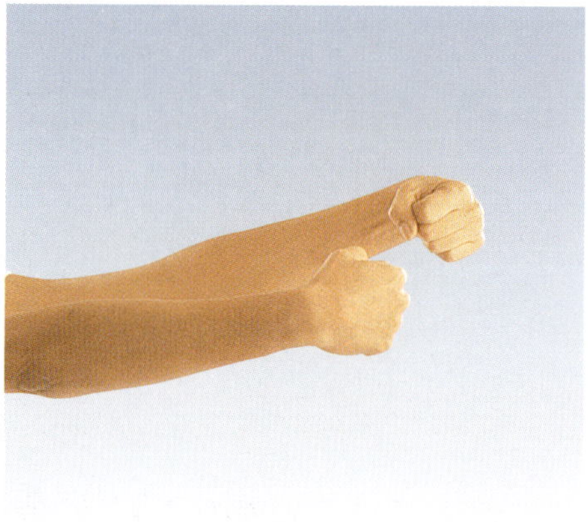

TADASANA VARIATION 1

PALM TREE POSTURE

1

Stand straight. Raise your hands straight upwards and interlock your fingers. Turn your palms upwards.

2

Raise your arms and back upwards and rise on to your toes. Focus on a particular point for balance. Hold the posture for 10-30 seconds.

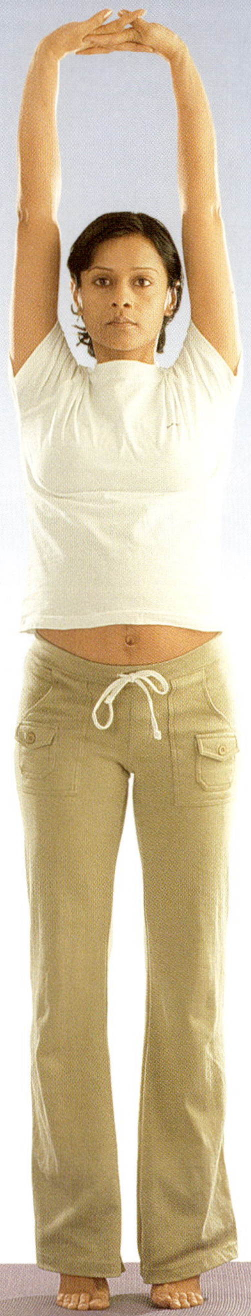

BENEFITS

Stretches and strengthens the back, thus preventing the occurrence of slipped disc and other back muscle spasms during pregnancy.

Stretches the entire body from head to toe and tones the muscles.

Stretches the rectus abdomini muscles and intestines which is required during the first six months of pregnancy.

TADASANA

PALM TREE POSTURE

BENEFITS

Stretches and strengthens the back, thus preventing the occurrence of slipped disc and other back muscle spasms during pregnancy.

Stretches the entire body from head to toe and tones the muscles.

Stretches the rectus abdomini muscles and intestines which is required during the first six months of pregnancy.

1

Stand straight. Raise your hands straight out to the sides.

2

Raise your hands straight upwards and join your palms. Stretch your arms and back to the top. Hold the posture for 10-30 seconds.

TIRYAKA TADASANA

SWAYING PALM TREE POSTURE

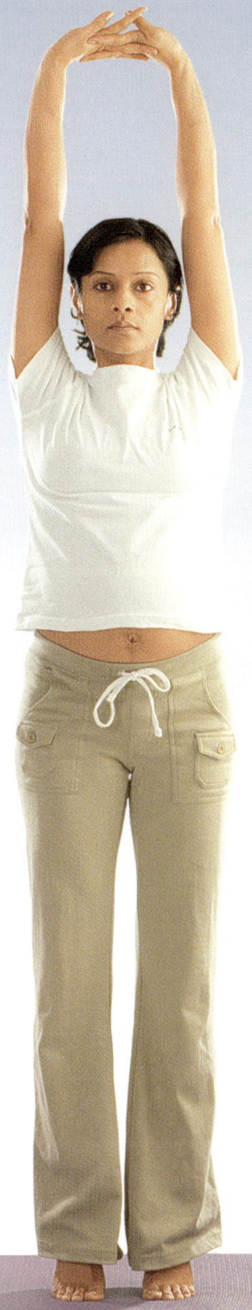

1

Perform *tadasana.*

2

Bend your body to one side and drop your heels to the floor. Hold the posture for 10-30 seconds.

Repeat on the opposite side.

BENEFITS

Stretches and strengthens the back, thus preventing the occurrence of slipped disc and other back muscle spasms during pregnancy.

Stretches the entire body from head to toe and tones the muscles.

Stretches the rectus abdominii muscles and intestines which is required during the first six months of pregnancy.

Stretches and exercises the muscles of the side of the torso to aid in taking the load during pregnancy.

CAUTION

Avoid holding your breath in this posture.

BENEFITS

Beneficial to correct postural problems.

Tones the waist, back, and hips which will take an immense load in the coming months.

Relieves back stiffness and pain.

KATI CHAKRASANA

WAIST ROTATING POSTURE

1

Stand straight with your neck relaxed. Bend your elbows. Place one palm on the opposite shoulder and place the other hand behind your back.

2

Turn your back and head in the direction of your hand at the back. Look backwards. Hold the posture for 10-30 seconds. Repeat by interchanging the position of your hands.

STANDING BHUJANGASANA

STANDING COBRA POSTURE

BENEFITS

Stretches the abdominal muscles.

Strengthens the muscles of the back to take the load during pregnancy.

Counters the forward pull of the abdominal area providing postural relief.

1

Stand straight. Fold your hands and place the palms on your hips.

2

Bend your back, shoulders, and head backwards and push your hips slightly forward. Hold for as long as is comfortable.

DWIKONASANA

DOUBLE ANGLE POSTURE

BENEFITS

Corrects posture and strengthens muscles of the back which is required during pregnancy.

Stretches the abdominal area and massages the internal organs and systems in the region.

Strengthens the shoulders, arms, chest, and neck which will all be required to lift the baby.

CAUTION

Avoid this posture if there is acute pain in the shoulder joints.

1

Stand straight with your neck relaxed.

2

Take your hands to the back and with one hand hold the wrist of your other hand.

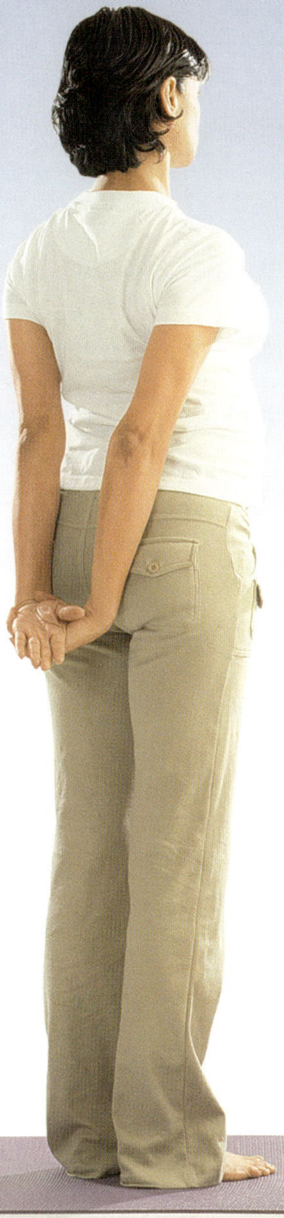

3

Straighten your elbows and draw your shoulders together.

4

Pull your shoulders back, bend your back slightly backwards, push your chest out, and look upwards. Hold the posture for 10-30 seconds.

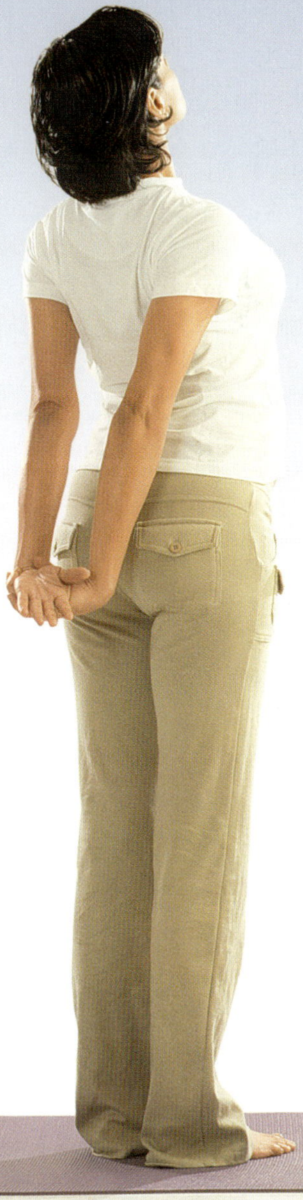

BENEFITS

Stretches the hamstrings and calf muscles.

Tones the sides, causing loss of weight.

Massages the internal organs of the abdominal area.

Stretches the back, especially the sides of the back and shoulders.

All of this strengthens the body to take the additional load in the coming months.

TRIKONASANA

TRIANGLE POSTURE

1

Stand straight with your hands by your hips.

2

Bend one elbow and place your palm over your shoulder, on the back. Gently bend your body to the opposite side and slide the opposite hand down your thigh. Hold the posture for 10-30 seconds. Repeat on the other side.

VAJRASANA

THUNDERBOLT POSTURE

1

Sit straight with your legs stretched straight out.

2

Fold one leg and bring your foot towards your hip. Place the instep of your foot under your buttock so that the weight is balanced on your ankle.

3

Bring the other foot under your buttock. Now your body rests on your ankles and instep of your feet. Place your hands on your thighs and sit comfortably with your back and head straight. Hold for as long as is comfortable.

BENEFITS

It is an important posture to relax the entire body and mind in preparation for pregnancy.

Improves the digestive process, alleviating ailments of the stomach.

Straightens the posture and strengthens the back muscles.

CAUTION

Avoid holding this posture for too long if your ankles are not able to bear your weight.

BHADRASANA

GRACIOUS POSTURE

BENEFITS

Strengthens the back which takes a huge load during pregnancy.

Increases the efficiency of the digestive process, relieving stomach ailments.

Tones and strengthens the thighs and hips which also carry an enormous weight during pregnancy.

Assists you in labour and alleviates menstrual disorders.

CAUTION

Those with knee injuries should avoid this posture.

1

Sit straight with your legs stretched straight out. Fold one leg and bring your foot towards your hip. Place the instep of your foot under your buttock so the weight is balanced on your ankle.

A child's well-being is rooted in the mother's well-being. If she is at peace, so is the child.

THE MASTER'S VOICE

2

Bring the other foot under your buttock. Now your body rests on your ankles and instep of your feet. Place your hands on your thighs and sit comfortably with your back and head straight.

3

Now draw your knees apart and sit with your back straight. Hold the posture for 10-30 seconds.

MERU WAKRASANA

SPINAL TWIST

BENEFITS

Relieves back pain, loosens the vertebrae, and tones the spinal nerves.

CAUTION

Those with severe back conditions or ulcer should avoid this posture.

1

Sit straight with your legs stretched out.

2

Fold one leg and cross it over your other thigh.

Moving through asanas teaches us to remain centred in the changing rhythms of life.

THE MASTER'S VOICE

3

Hold your bent knee and place the other hand straight at the back on the floor. Gently turn your back and look over your shoulder. Hold the posture for 10-30 seconds. Repeat with your other leg.

GOMUKHASANA

COW FACE POSTURE

BENEFITS

Induces the right posture during pregnancy by opening the chest area, and relieves backache, and sciatica.

Induces relaxation and removes tiredness and anxiety.

Stimulates the kidneys.

CAUTION

Release the hold if the muscles in the arms begin to hurt.

1

Sit in *vajrasana* (see p. 161).

2

Fold one elbow and take your hand to your back from above your shoulder. Keep your elbow beside your head.

3

Fold your other elbow and bring your hand from underneath. Interlock the fingers of your two hands.

4

Sit with your back straight and push your head slightly backwards to stretch the hand to your back. Then repeat the practice by interchanging the position of the hands. Hold the posture for 10-30 seconds.

PADMASANA

LOTUS POSTURE

BENEFITS

Padmasana stabilizes the body and stills the mind. Practising sitting still and meditating for a few minutes daily will help reduce the tension and trauma that accompanies childbirth.

Strengthens the back muscles and straightens the posture for pregnancy.

Releases excess gas from the abdominal area.

CAUTION

Ensure that you alternate the position of your legs.

1

Sit with your back straight and your feet stretched out.

3

Place your foot on your thigh as close to the groin as possible.

2

Fold one leg and bring your foot towards your groin.

4

Fold the other leg and place your foot on your bent leg as close as possible to the groin. Sit with your back and head straight and place your hands on your knees. Hold the posture for as long as is comfortable.

TITLIASANA

BUTTERFLY POSTURE

BENEFITS

Opens up the groin and inner thighs, thus providing relaxation and reducing the pain during labour.

Strengthens the back muscles to take the load during pregnancy.

1

Sit down with your back straight. Fold your legs and join your feet.

2

Bring your feet close to your groin and interlock your hands around them.

3

Move your legs up and down in a continuous flapping motion. Continue for 10-30 seconds.

UTTANASANA

SQUAT AND RISE POSTURE

1

Sit on your haunches with your knees wide apart and your body bending forward, balanced by your hands.

2

Raise your hands off the floor and interlock them. Straighten your back and raise your shoulders.

3

Turn your wrists to face your palms downwards. Hold the posture for 10-30 seconds.

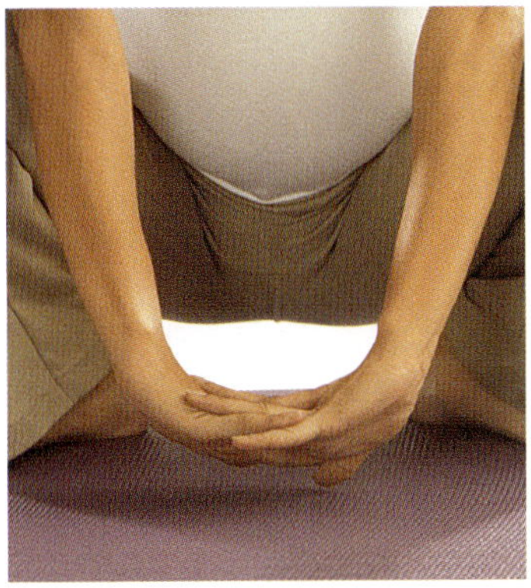

BENEFITS

Strengthens the muscles of the back for the months of pregnancy.

Strengthens the pelvis and uterus which helps to reduce labour pain.

Stretches and strengthens the groin and inner thighs.

CAUTION

After the third month of pregnancy, avoid sitting on the haunches. Instead, stop about 30 cm above the ground.

MARJARIASANA

CAT STRETCH POSTURE

BENEFITS

Makes the back and neck supple and flexible for a painless delivery.

Forces the body to bring focus and co-ordination between breath and movement.

1

Sit in *vajrasana* (see p. 161). Raise yourself onto your knees and drop your hands to the floor so that your back is parallel to the floor.

2

Inhale and bend your back and head upwards.

3

Exhale and round your back. Bend your back and head inwards. Repeat a few times.

SETHUBANDASANA

BRIDGE POSTURE

BENEFITS

Stretches the abdominal area and internal organs.

Gives a mild stretch to the back.

Strengthens the thighs and shoulders to take the load during pregnancy.

CAUTION

Do not practise this posture if you have weak wrists or high blood pressure.

Avoid practising beyond the fourth month if you experience pain.

1

Lie flat on your back and fold your knees. Place your legs close to your buttocks.

2

Gently raise your hips off the floor.

3

Raise your hips and back further off the floor till your body is in a straight line from knee to neck. Hold the posture for 10-30 seconds.

JALANDHAR BANDHA

THROAT LOCK

BENEFITS

Regulates the functioning of the thyroid gland and metabolism.

Causes decreased heart rate and increased breath retention.

Relieves stress, anxiety, and anger, and helps in relaxation.

These benefits help in a stress-free delivery.

CAUTION

Those suffering from cervical spondylosis, high blood pressure, vertigo, and heart disease should avoid this posture.

1

Sit in *padmasana* (see p. 168). Take in a deep breath.

2

Retain the breath inside and lock your chin to your chest. Hold the breath for as long as possible. Then release the chin lock, raise your head and exhale. Practise this technique only three times.

MOOLA BANDHA

ROOT LOCK

1

Sit in a meditative posture with your back straight and hands on your knees.

BENEFITS

Regulates the functioning of the thyroid gland and metabolism.

Causes decreased heart rate and increased breath retention.

Relieves stress anxiety, and anger, and helps in relaxation.

These benefits help in a stress-free delivery.

2

Exhale completely. Raise the genital space and constrict the anal space. The abdominal muscles are tightened. Hold your breath outside for as long as is comfortable. Then release the lock and inhale. This can be performed only three times.

ANULOM VILOM PRANAYAMA

ALTERNATE NOSTRIL BREATHING

BENEFITS

The body absorbs a larger quantity of oxygen and expels carbon dioxide. This refreshes and revitalizes the body.

A state of tranquility is reached and the power to concentrate is enhanced.

Lowers stress and anxiety.

CAUTION

Those with high blood pressure should not hold their breath.

1

Sit comfortably with your legs folded and your back straight.

2

Open up the fist of your preferred hand. Fold your index and middle fingers. Close your eyes and practise deep breathing.

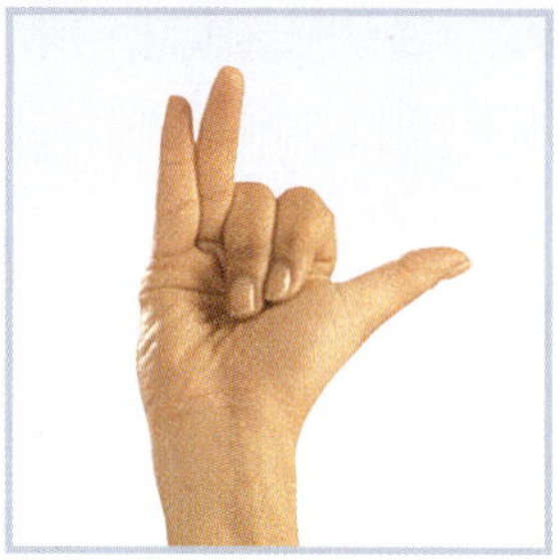

3

Block your right nostril with your thumb and place your ring finger between your eyebrows. Breathe in through your left nostril to a count of five.

4

Bring your ring finger to the left nostril and close it. Retain your breath inside for a count of ten.

5

Raise your thumb to between your eyebrows and exhale slowly through your right nostril to a count of ten. Once the exhalation has been completed, breathe in through the right nostril again to a count of five. Repeat the whole procedure, alternating between your left and right nostrils for about 2-5 minutes.

A child is like clay in the hands of a potter. Mud has no identity of its own, but the potter gives it structure and meaning.

Today's child suffers from the effects of modernization. A high-growth environment puts tremendous pressure on the child—he has to prove himself to parents, peers, friends, and teachers.

Yoga can give the child focus, awareness, sensitivity, relief from stress, freedom from loneliness, solace, and initiates the child on an inward journey.

If *yama* and *niyama* (the basic ethical codes of life such as satya and ahimsa) are taught from childhood, one can aim at making a perfect child, citizen, and human being. This will also help the child to adjust to his enviroment positively.

There are three types of asanas suitable for children—cultural, meditative, and relaxing—and they cater to different needs. Children should not practise pranayama excessively as their lungs are not fully developed. *Bandhas* will not affect children much as hormones are secreted only after puberty and their glands are not fully formed. *Kriyas* are for youngsters above the age of twelve. Mudras may be practised since they define moods.

Yoga benefits every child intellectually, emotionally, and physically. It can help a child to achieve balance in a fast-changing world and prepares him for a healthy adolescence.

YOGA FOR CHILDREN

TADASANA

PALM TREE POSTURE

Stand straight. Stretch your hands upwards and join your palms.

Stretch your back and hands upwards and rise on your toes.

BENEFITS

Helps to increase height by 1-2 inches since it strengthens and straightens the spine.

Stretches the abdominal area and internal organs, improving digestion. Good practice for overweight children.

Stretches the back, shoulders, and neck muscles.

STANDING BHUJANGASANA

STANDING COBRA POSTURE

Stand straight with your palms on your hips. Bend backwards and lower your head. Hold for as long as is comfortable. Repeat twice.

BENEFITS

Increases flexibility of the spine.

Strengthens the back and tones the abdominal muscles.

Relieves tension in the neck area.

CAUTION

This posture should be done slowly and for a short duration.

ARDHACHAKRASANA

HALF-WHEEL POSTURE

BENEFITS

Stretches the sides and removes excess weight. The stretching helps the growing child. Also helps children to lose weight.

Tones and massages the internal organs of the abdominal area.

Increases the respiratory capacity of the lung.

CAUTION

Do not hold your breath while holding the posture.

Stand straight. Raise one hand straight upwards beside your ear. Gently bend your body to one side by sliding the opposite hand down the thigh. Hold the posture for 10-30 seconds. Then repeat on the other side.

VRIKSHASANA

TREE POSTURE

BENEFITS

Strengthens the muscles of the legs and knees.

Straightens the spine and helps digestion and stomach ailments.

Develops balance of body and of mind, and enhances concentration.

CAUTION

Children with weak knees should hold this posture for short durations and gradually increase the duration.

Stand straight. Bend one knee and place your foot flat on the inner thigh of the opposite leg. Maintain balance by fixing your gaze on a point straight in front. Raise your hands straight upwards and join your palms. Stretch your back and hands upwards. Hold for as long as is comfortable. Then repeat with the other leg.

SWETASANA

SWAN POSTURE

BENEFITS

Stretches the back and alleviates mild backaches.

Stretches the thighs and calf muscles.

CAUTION

Overweight children and those with weak ankles should hold this posture for a short duration.

Stand straight. Bend your knees and lower your body till the buttocks are just above the floor. Your weight is balanced on your feet. Fold your elbows, rest your arms on your knees and place the palms against your cheeks. Hold the posture for 10-30 seconds.

VAJRASANA

THUNDERBOLT POSTURE

Sit with your legs outstretched and your back straight. Fold one leg and bring the ankle under your buttock. Fold the other leg and bring it under your other buttock, crossing only the big toes. Keep your back straight and your hands on your knees. Hold for as long as is comfortable.

BENEFITS

Develops the strength of the back by ensuring it is kept straight.

Improves digestion and alleviates ailments of the stomach such as constipation, hyperacidity and peptic ulcer.

Induces a state of stillness in the body that is required to concentrate, to grasp lessons.

CAUTION

Children with injured knees or ankles should avoid this posture.

BENEFITS

Strengthens the inner thighs

This posture opens up the hip joint and groin. Opening the groin reduces the child's accumulated stress and phobias.

TITLIASANA

BUTTERFLY POSTURE

Sit straight with your legs stretched out. Fold your knees and draw the feet towards your groin. Interlock your hands around your feet and keep your back straight. Move your legs continuously up and down in a flapping motion. Continue for 1-2 minutes.

PADMASANA
LOTUS POSTURE

Sit straight with your legs stretched out. Fold one knee and place your foot on the opposite thigh, close to your groin. Fold the other leg and place it over the bent thigh. Pull your foot towards the groin. Keep your back straight and place your hands on your knees. Hold for as long as is comfortable.

BENEFITS

Strengthens the legs.

Straightens the spine.

Steadies the mind and helps improve concentration. This is essential for children to study.

Stimulates digestion.

CAUTION

Children with weak ankles should practise this for 10-15 seconds and gradually increase duration upto a minute.

BAITHAK PARVATASANA

SEATED MOUNTAIN POSTURE

BENEFITS

Stretches and pulls the back upwards. Helps to stretch the spine which is vital for the growing child.

Stretches and strengthens the muscles of the neck and shoulders.

Stretches and tones the abdomen and massages the internal organs of the stomach area, alleviating alimentary disorders.

1

Sit with your legs crossed and your back straight. Raise your hands straight upwards and join your palms.

2

Stretch your back and look upwards.

PADAHASTASANA

HAND-TO-FOOT POSTURE

Stand straight. Raise your hands straight upwards. Exhale and bend your body downwards with your back stretched. Touch your toes with your fingers and look down. Breathe normally. Hold the posture for 10-30 seconds.

BENEFITS

Stretches and tones the hamstring and calf muscles.

Stretches the muscles of the back and neck.

Helps overweight children to lose weight.

CAUTION

Children with severe back conditions such as slipped disc should avoid this posture.

HASTA BHOONAMAN ASANA

HAND-TO-GROUND POSTURE

BENEFITS

Stretches and tones the hamstrings and calf muscles.

Creates a mild stretch for the inner thighs.

Improves the flexibility of the back.

Stand with your legs wide apart. Raise your hands straight upwards. Exhaling, start bending your body downwards with your back stretched. Drop your fingers to the floor and look forward. Hold the posture for 10-30 seconds.

PARVATASANA

MOUNTAIN POSTURE

Stand straight. Raise your hands straight upwards. Exhale and bend your body with your back stretched. Place the palms on the floor and push your upper body inwards, looking at the navel. Try to touch your heels to the floor. Breathe normally. Hold the posture for 10-30 seconds.

BENEFITS

Stretches and tones the hamstrings and calf muscles.

Stretches the muscles of the back and neck.

Strengthens the hands and shoulders.

CAUTION

Children with severe back pain and spasms should be careful while attempting this posture.

PASCHIMOTTANASANA

BACK STRETCH POSTURE

BENEFITS

Stretches and tones the back, hamstrings, and calf muscles.

Enriches blood supply to the spine.

Tones abdominal muscles and organs which helps in digestion, and helps lose excess weight.

Sit straight with your legs stretched out. Raise your hands straight upwards. Exhale and bend your back downwards. Reach out and hold your toes with your fingers. Pull yourself downwards and look down. Breathe normally. Hold the posture for 10-30 seconds.

JANUSIRSASANA

HEAD-TO-KNEE POSTURE

Sit straight with your legs stretched out. Fold one knee and bring the foot to the groin placing your knee on the floor. Raise your hands straight upwards. Exhale and bend your back. Hold the toes of your outstretched leg with your fingers and pull yourself downwards. Look down. Hold the posture for 10-30 seconds. Repeat with the other leg.

BENEFITS

Stretches the hamstrings and flexes the hip joints.

Tones the internal organs of the abdominal area and helps lose excess weight.

Enhances stimulation of the nerves and strengthens muscles of the spine.

Helps in alleviating bronchial conditions.

BHUJANGASANA

COBRA POSTURE

BENEFITS

Alleviates backache.

Regular practice keeps the spine healthy.

This posture has a positive effect on the nervous system.

This is beneficial for the liver and kidneys.

CAUTION

Children who have a hyper-active thyroid should avoid this posture.

Lie flat on your stomach. Place the palms on the floor beside your shoulders. Raise your head, shoulders, and back upwards and straighten your arms. Hold the posture for as long as is comfortable.

DHANURASANA
BOW POSTURE

Lie flat on your stomach. Fold your knees and bring your feet to the buttocks. Grasp your ankles with your hands. Raise your legs, shoulders, and back upwards and look upwards. Hold the posture for 10-30 seconds.

BENEFITS

The spinal column is stretched, improving blood circulation to the spinal nerves.

The chest area is expanded increasing breathing capacity, hence helps in the treatment of asthma and other chest ailments, which children often contract.

Helps in the correction of hunching of the shoulders and spine.

CAUTION

Children suffering from any irregular heart or lung conditions should not perform this posture.

USHTRASANA

CAMEL POSTURE

BENEFITS

By stretching the stomach and abdominal area it stimulates the digestive system and alleviates constipation.

Alleviates backache, drooping shoulders, and rounded back conditions which are quite common in children.

CAUTION

Children with extreme thyroid conditions should do this only after expert guidance.

Sit in *vajrasana* (see p. 187). Raise your body and kneel down with your legs apart. Drop your hands to the ankles and bend your back and head downwards. Push your hips outwards. Hold for as long as is comfortable. To return, raise one hand off the ankle and then the next and raise your back up. Return to *vajrasana*.

CHAKRASANA

WHEEL POSTURE

Lie flat on your back. Bend your elbows and place your palms on the floor touching your shoulders, with fingers pointing towards the neck. Bend your knees and place feet close to the buttocks. In sequence raise your hips, shoulders, and head off the floor by supporting the weight on your hands and legs.

Straighten your elbows, raise your hips higher, stretch your back completely and push your stomach outwards. Hold the posture for as long as is comfortable.

Return to the floor slowly by lowering your shoulders and then your back without any strain on the back.

BENEFITS

Stretches the stomach and is beneficial to the digestive and respiratory systems.

Strengthens the back and makes it flexible and supple.

Strengthens the shoulders which take the weight off the body.

CAUTION

Those with weak wrists, and overweight children should avoid this posture.

This should be avoided during illness.

THE 41-DAY TRANSFORMATION

KAYAKALP

Man has been working endlessly to acquire a level of comfort that allows him to work the very least and 'live' the most. Today, he has stopped believing in himself and believes in his own creation—the computer. Even for a simple arithmetic calculation, he needs assistance. The mind continues to create new things, but this has brought him no mental peace; only speed and stress. He has forgotten that at one point this effort was made so that he could pause and enjoy his creation.

REVERSING THE AGEING PROCESS

Our ancestors researched into reversing the aging process and they called it Kayakalp. *Kaya* means body and *Kalp* means re-doing. Kayakalp is a beautiful system of regenerating the whole body, which involves reliving and changing habits and lifestyle in all aspects—physical, mental, emotional, and spiritual. Lastly, it gives the ability to flush out toxins generated by poor eating and lifestyle habits.

Kayakalp is a beautifully researched system by which it is possible to reverse the age of the body from 50 to 35 years. In the past, when Indian masters felt that they had aged, they practised the process of Kayakalp for a year. At the end of this, they had a new body, which would last for another ten years.

Today, the year-long process of Kayakalp is difficult to sustain. There are many personal, as well as social constraints that may hinder the practice of Kayakalp for one full year. Instead, you can apply the following segment of Kayakalp for 41 days and regenerate your body. Your new and rejuvenated body will last you for six months.

41 DAYS

1. The first thing you need to do if you want to enter this system of reversing the ageing process is to disconnect yourself from urban life. Go to a remote place where people don't know you and will let you live the way you wish to. Understand that it is a process of bringing the focus from the world of success, the world of attachment, the world of fear, the world of insecurity, the world of dependency and the world of regret and guilt, to a world of inward self growth.

Kayakalp is only for those people who accept that they can change and are willing to do something to make it happen. That is all the qualification required to enter the process of Kayakalp.

2. All your relatives, those who bother you and those who are not there in your life anymore, have to be left behind for 41 days. This needs to be done because in your present world, it is not only you who are responsible for the negative energies inside. People around you aggravate those energies and you think whatever is right is your achievement and whatever is wrong, is created by others.

In this space around you, you will be able to accept your mental state as it is. In these 41 days you will develop an understanding that there is nothing such as negative energy. There is, however, something called negative response. The response mechanism has to change from fighting to acceptance, and from holding to letting go. The result may stun peple who have known you ealier.

Kayakalp is a mental leap from the polarities of understanding and misunderstanding to a state of surrender. You don't have to be spiritual to practise Kayakalp but you should be an experimentalist to go into it.

3. You have to work on all kinds of habits here because habits bring in mental dependency. They make you weak and so you age faster. Any kind of mental dependency has to be left behind. If you drink, smoke, think or live in a relationship out of habit, disconnect for 41 days. If too much sleep is your habit, then just sleep 5-7 hours a day for these 41 days.

4. Guilt and fear is another area of work in Kayakalp. As you know, nothing in this world moves without His wish and nothing up to now has been done by you without His wish. So why carry guilt. Guilt is nothing but an attack on your belief system. Each man creates a world of belief around himself. Fear and guilt are the edges on which you live everyday in your self-created belief system. It is not that Kayakalp is talking about a life of indulgence. It talks about a new man whose sole wish in life is to say, 'I am happy for this moment.' So whatever gets in the way of your happiness, avoid doing it. My motive in writing this is that Kayakalp should work so well for you that you don't come out of it for the rest of your life.

5.You need to be with nature. Find a place preferably near water—at a beach or in the mountains, or take a room in a jungle resort or in a remote village.

AGNISAR KRIYA
Activating the Digestive Fire

Sit in *vajrasana* and separate your knees as far as is possible. Place your hands on the knees and close your eyes. Take in a few deep breaths and relax your body, especially the abdominal muscles. Push forward slightly, so that your elbows are straightened. Empty your lungs completely. Perform *jalandhara bandha* (see p. 100). Contract and expand the abdominal muscles while keeping the breath outside. Release *jalandhara bandha*. Take in a deep breath. This is one round. Let the breathing normalize. Practise three rounds of ten contractions each to begin with. Then gradually increase that to 100 contractions. The ability to retain the breath outside will improve with time. Also the control over the abdominal muscles will improve.

PRECAUTIONS: Should be practised in the morning on an empty stomach.
BENEFITS: Stimulates the appetite and removes digestive disorders such as indigestion, hyperacidity, constipation, flatulence, and sluggishness of the liver and kidneys. Remedies sluggishness, depression, and lethargy
CAUTION: People suffering from high blood pressure, heart disease, duodenal or peptic ulcers, a thyroid disorder, and chronic diarrhoea should avoid this posture. Women over three months pregnant should avoid this posture.

KUNJAL KRIYA
Regurgitative Cleansing

PREPARATION: Add 2 tsp of salt to about 2 lt of lukewarm water.

Stand near a sink or outside in the garden. Drink at least 6 glasses of the prepared water at one stretch. Ensure that you gulp down the water and not sip it slowly. Stand with your legs apart and your back bent forward. Place the index and middle fingers in the mouth (ensure that your hand is clean and nails are cut) and rub the back of the tongue down. This stimulates the vomiting process. The water will start coming out of the mouth. Wait till all the water comes out. If the vomiting stops, again rub the back of the tongue with your fingers. Ensure that all the water comes out. Then relax for a while and practise deep breathing.

PRECAUTIONS: Should be practised in the morning on an empty stomach.
Should be practised once a week to clean the system.
BENEFITS: Tones the abdominal organs, removing indigestion, acidity, and gas. Excess mucus is removed, helping to remedy cold, cough, bronchitis, and asthma. It helps to release pent-up emotions and blocks, or heaviness in the heart caused by inner and outer conflict.
CAUTION: Should be avoided by people suffering from hernia, high blood pressure, heart disease, stroke, acute peptic ulcer or diabetics with eye problems.

JALANETI KRIYA
Nasal Cleansing with Water

PREPARATION: A special *neti lota—'-neti pot'* should be used. It resembles a teapot with one end as a nozzle. The end should not be too thick or pointed. It should fit comfortably in the nostril. Prepare lukewarm water by adding 1 tsp salt per half litre.

Stand with your legs apart and bend slightly forward. Tilt your head forward and to one side. Practise deep breathing. Place the end of the nozzle in the nostril that is facing upwards. Let the water flow slowly into the nostril. Do not force. Slowly the water will enter the nostril and flow out through the other nostril. When the water is over, straighten your head and blow gently to remove excess mucus. Then repeat in the other nostril. When you have finished, dry your nostrils by performing *kapalbathi kriya* with one nostril closed and then the other for 3 minutes.

BENEFITS: Removes mucus and pollution from the nasal passage and sinuses. Prevents respiratory tract diseases such as asthma, pneumonia, bronchitis, and pulmonary tuberculosis. Relieves disorders of the ears, eyes, and throat including myopia, allergic rhinitis, hay fever, tonsillitis. Relieves muscular tension in the face and maintains a youthful appearance. Alleviates anxiety, anger, and depression. Helps remove drowsiness and generally improves the activities of the brain and overall health.
CAUTION: Should be avoided by people suffering from chronic nose-bleeds.

THE PROCESS

DAY 1	Wear thin, loose-fitting cotton clothes. Clean up the place in which you are planning to spend the 41 days. Sit down after every *kriya* and chant: 'I will finish it, I will finish it. And I am happy for myself now.' Chant at least for an hour every 3-4 hours. Say, 'Thank God' in the course of doing everything. Like 'Thank God I could take out time to go into Kayakalp', 'Thank God I have food to eat' and 'Thank God I have a bed to sleep on.' These 41 days are nothing but working your state of mind and being.
DAY 2	Spend a lot of time outside your room. Go for a 3 km walk in the morning. After that, take a cold shower and listen to any music that relaxes you or sit at a place where you can hear birds chirping or water falling and be aware of the sounds around. Doing this develops sensitivity. For food, have just fruits, as much as you want, but seasonal and fresh. In the evening, go for a stroll in the jungle, or by the sea or for a hike in the hills.
DAY 3	Wake up and stretch your body in bed—what you naturally do when you wake up. Do this for half an hour. Follow this with honey-ginger-lemon tea, and a 3 km walk. On return, write down the names of everyone you know in your life with a small note on what you know about that person—good or bad. If you get tired, sit at a beautiful spot outside and relax. In the evening, sit down in your room. Light some candles (aroma or incense sticks, if available). Lie down on your back, inhale and exhale and observe the movement of your stomach. Have a light meal before you go to bed.
DAYS 4 TO 11	Stretch on the bed followed by herbal tea, fruits and the walk. Take the paper on which you wrote out the names of the people in your life. Recall all those people who have harmed you, for whom you have negative feelings. Seek strength from God for forgiveness and let them go out of your system. Continue this for a week. In the evening have a light meal. (During the day, have as much fruit as you want.) Do not rush. There will be only a few people who would have had a negative impact on you. This negative impact will take its own time to get released from your head. At night, don't forget to say, 'Thanks, you have harmed me, but I am better now. I am happy and I have forgiven you now.'

DAYS 12 TO 18

Food—tea in the morning followed by one fruit, preferably an apple or two oranges or two guavas. Lunch—boiled vegetables, salads and soup. Dinner—one good vegetarian meal, not too heavy. Activities for the following week—on waking up, stretches and the *merudandasana* (see p. 70) sequence, followed by *kunjal kriya* (see p. 205). Sit down and concentrate on relaxed breathing throughout the day. Try and focus your mind on breathing. Even if the mind gets bored, try and come back to the breathing. To take a break, go out for some time.

In the evening, go for a walk, and follow it up with ten rounds of *surya namaskar* (see p. 18) or less depending on your capacity. Continue this for another 6 days. Drink as much water as possible because you are approaching the breathing practices. Consume at least 5 litres of water daily, so that toxins can be washed out of your body.

DAYS 19 TO 26

First thing in the morning have *triphal churan* (1 tsp of *Bar Ahad Amla* combination in water). Drink of the day—lemon water with a little sugar and salt. Food—6 to 10 bananas a day. No more *kunjal kriya*.

Perform *jalaneti* (see p. 205) and *kapalabhati kriya* (see p. 98). *Agnisar kriya* (see p. 204) three times a day. Pick up a mala and chant *'Aum'* for 5 rounds (of the mala) with eyes closed. In the evening, a 5 km walk followed by 15 rounds of *surya namaskar*. Continue this for one week.

DAYS 27 TO 37

Consume *chirauta* herb to purify your blood early morning followed by a walk and *surya namaskar*. Perform all the three *bandhas* during the day. Switch on music, close your eyes and perform lots of slow movements and bring awareness to your body. Avoid any unwanted movements. Enjoy the space of the void or emptiness. Keep chanting *'Aum'* throughout the day and practise *anulom vilom pranayama* (see p. 178) for half an hour every day.

Continue this for the next 10 days.

DAYS 38 TO 41

Have a regular, light breakfast. Do one hour of breathing exercise. *Surya namaskar*—25 rounds. Walk 6-8 km. Lunch should also be closer to regular food but less oily and less spicy. Continue the rest of the practice.

INDEX

ASANAS

PRANAYAMA

BANDHAS

KRIYAS

MUDRAS